Family Violence

Other Books in the Current Controversies Series:

Family
Violence

J.D. Lloyd, *Book Editor*

David Bender, *Publisher*
Bruno Leone, *Executive Editor*

Bonnie Szumski, *Editorial Director*
Stuart Miller, *Managing Editor*

CURRENT CONTROVERSIES

Cover photo: © Tony Stone Images/Claudia Kunin

Library of Congress Cataloging-in-Publication Data

Family violence / J.D. Lloyd, book editor.
    p. cm. — (Current controversies)
    Includes bibliographical references and index.
    ISBN 0-7377-0451-9 (pbk) — ISBN 0-7377-0452-7 (lib)
    1. Family violence—United States. I. Lloyd, J.D., 1959–   . II. Series.

HV6626.2 .F348   2001
362.82'92'0973—dc21   00-027984
                                                                CIP

©2001 by Greenhaven Press, Inc., PO Box 289009, San Diego, CA 92198-9009
Printed in the U.S.A.

Contents

Chapter 1: Who Are the Victims of Family Violence?

Domestic violence is the leading cause of injury to women in the United
States. Domestic violence takes many forms, such as beating, choking,
and rape, and it need not be physical in nature. Batterers, who possess an
exaggerated sense of entitlement, control their victims through coercive
tactics that resemble those used by Nazi guards in the death camps.

A 1980 study of 860 men and women found that women report using
violence in their relationships more often than men, and that women do
not only hit in response to their partners' attacks. Since this study was
released, researchers have avoided acknowledging the fact that men are
often victims of domestic violence. However, new data dispels the stereotype that spouse abuse is only a problem for women.

Child maltreatment takes many forms, including neglect, physical injury,
sexual abuse, and emotional abuse. During the 1980s, reports of child
abuse in the United States increased by 200 percent, and current estimates
suggest that between 2 and 3 percent of children experience some form of
abuse. Although bruises, burns, black eyes, and other physical signs of
abuse may be present, child abuse often goes undetected or unreported.

The abuse of elderly family members is a pervasive problem. Elderly
parents are frequently cared for by single, divorced, or widowed daughters who are also in their retirement years, and who may feel resentment
and frustration regarding responsibility for their elderly parent. Elder
abuse takes many forms, such as beating, humiliation, neglect, and
exploitation of financial resources. Elderly men are as likely as elderly
women to be abused.

Chapter 2: Is the Prevalence of Family Violence Exaggerated?

Yes: The Prevalence of Family Violence Is Exaggerated

No: Family Violence Is Not Exaggerated

Chapter 3: What Are the Causes of Family Violence?

Chapter 4: How Can Family Violence Be Reduced?

Stronger Efforts Are Needed to Reduce Family Violence

aware that domestic abuse involves domination and control—it is not "mutual combat." The motivations and characteristics of batterers can be profiled just like those of serial rapists and murderers. By understanding the patterns that often characterize domestic violence, officers can better protect victims from repeated abuse.

In order to effectively address the issue of domestic violence, religious leaders must first ensure that their traditions are not oppressive to church members. They can then make the church a safe place to address domestic violence through the use of sermons, Sunday school classes, and outside speakers that cover the subject. Religious leaders must also be aware of their limitations, however, and refer women to the appropriate secular resources, such as hotlines and shelters, when necessary.

Some Efforts to Reduce Family Violence Are Ineffective

Laws that require physicians to report domestic violence remove health care professionals' ability to decide on a case-by-case basis what is best for a patient. These blanket policies are ineffective in assisting the victim, whose needs are highly individual and complex. Simply reporting the suspected abuse without arranging for protection may place the victim back in the hands of a batterer made even more angry by the reporting.

Mandatory arrest policies and restraining orders are ineffective solutions to the problem of domestic violence because they are rarely followed up with the criminal sanctions necessary to protect the victim. No studies have demonstrated that restraining orders are usually obeyed or that mandatory arrest policies reduce domestic violence. In fact, data from the National Institute of Justice indicates that these policies may often enrage batterers and encourage rather than deter violence.

Religious communities may sometimes condone or even encourage abusive behavior by parents. Indeed, discipline is required many times by religious teachings when children violate religious norms. Religious practices may even endorse "punishments," such as beating with rods, that most lay persons would view as torture. The insularity of the religious community can prevent the abuse from being recognized by outsiders who could help.

Foreword

By definition, controversies are "discussions of questions in which opposing opinions clash" (Webster's Twentieth Century Dictionary Unabridged). Few would deny that controversies are a pervasive part of the human condition and exist on virtually every level of human enterprise. Controversies transpire between individuals and among groups, within nations and between nations. Controversies supply the grist necessary for progress by providing challenges and challengers to the status quo. They also create atmospheres where strife and warfare can flourish. A world without controversies would be a peaceful world; but it also would be, by and large, static and prosaic.

The Series' Purpose

The purpose of the Current Controversies series is to explore many of the social, political, and economic controversies dominating the national and international scenes today. Titles selected for inclusion in the series are highly focused and specific. For example, from the larger category of criminal justice, Current Controversies deals with specific topics such as police brutality, gun control, white collar crime, and others. The debates in Current Controversies also are presented in a useful, timeless fashion. Articles and book excerpts included in each title are selected if they contribute valuable, long-range ideas to the overall debate. And wherever possible, current information is enhanced with historical documents and other relevant materials. Thus, while individual titles are current in focus, every effort is made to ensure that they will not become quickly outdated. Books in the Current Controversies series will remain important resources for librarians, teachers, and students for many years.

In addition to keeping the titles focused and specific, great care is taken in the editorial format of each book in the series. Book introductions and chapter prefaces are offered to provide background material for readers. Chapters are organized around several key questions that are answered with diverse opinions representing all points on the political spectrum. Materials in each chapter include opinions in which authors clearly disagree as well as alternative opinions in which authors may agree on a broader issue but disagree on the possible solutions. In this way, the content of each volume in Current Controversies mirrors the mosaic of opinions encountered in society. Readers will quickly realize that there are many viable answers to these complex issues. By questioning each author's conclusions, students and casual readers can begin to develop the critical thinking skills so important to evaluating opinionated material.

Current Controversies is also ideal for controlled research. Each anthology in the series is composed of primary sources taken from a wide gamut of informational categories including periodicals, newspapers, books, United States and foreign government documents, and the publications of private and public organizations. Readers will find factual support for reports, debates, and research papers covering all areas of important issues. In addition, an annotated table of contents, an index, a book and periodical bibliography, and a list of organizations to contact are included in each book to expedite further research.

Perhaps more than ever before in history, people are confronted with diverse and contradictory information. During the Persian Gulf War, for example, the public was not only treated to minute-to-minute coverage of the war, it was also inundated with critiques of the coverage and countless analyses of the factors motivating U.S. involvement. Being able to sort through the plethora of opinions accompanying today's major issues, and to draw one's own conclusions, can be a complicated and frustrating struggle. It is the editors' hope that Current Controversies will help readers with this struggle.

Introduction

In his book *Wounded Innocents*, writer Richard Wexler recounts the testimony of eight-year-old Mary Ellen Wilson in the first U.S. court case concerning child abuse. The year was 1874:

> Mama has been in the habit of whipping and beating me almost every day. She used to whip me with a twisted whip, a raw hide. The whip always left a black and blue mark on my body. I have now the black and blue marks on my head which were made by mama, and also a cut on the left side of my forehead which was made by a pair of scissors. She struck me with the scissors and cut me . . . I do not know for what I was whipped—mama never said anything to me when she whipped me.

Interestingly, this case was brought before the court by the American Society for the Prevention of Cruelty to Animals (ASPCA). Although there had been laws enacted as early as colonial times to prevent child abuse, in practice the legal system had mostly ignored the issue. In Mary Ellen's case, the ASPCA successfully argued that the girl was protected under laws barring the mistreatment of animals.

As a result of the publicity surrounding Mary Ellen's case, more than two hundred Societies for the Prevention of Cruelty to Children sprang up around the country, and many states passed laws making child abuse illegal. However, public awareness of the problem wavered over the next eighty years, and child abuse remained a largely unacknowledged fact of life in America. Most communities continued to expect the family itself to deal with the issue; if anyone did intercede on the behalf of the victim, it was likely to be an extended family member or a pastor, and the problem was unlikely to be reported. Children were rarely removed from any but the poorest families.

Historically, authorities got involved only when violence resulted in severe physical injury or death. The passage of the first mandatory child abuse reporting laws at the state level in the early 1960s began a transformation of the issue—from a taboo family secret to a social problem worthy of academic debate. As reports came in from doctors and teachers, the public's willingness to address the issue on a national level coalesced, and in 1974 Congress passed the Child Abuse Prevention and Treatment Act (CAPTA). The act, which earmarked federal funds for states that passed mandatory child abuse reporting laws, has encouraged the passage of such laws in all fifty states.

Just as child victims of family violence once suffered in silence, so did most women victims. Researcher Del Martin writes that battered wives often remained isolated "as a result of our society's almost tangible contempt for female victims of violence." Prevailing societal attitudes allowed for a certain acceptance of wife-beating—it was seen as a man's right as head of the household. Although some states enacted laws against spouse abuse, the crime was frequently difficult to prove, and the courts usually erred on the side of the defendant. As was the case with child abuse, authorities mostly stayed out of what was perceived as "family business."

The growing awareness of child abuse and the emerging feminism of the 1960s laid the groundwork for a public acknowledgement of wife abuse. Early crusaders of the "battered women's movement," who sought to give voice to the oppressed by setting up victims' shelters and speaking out about the issue, initially met with stiff resistance from traditionalists. Researcher Andrew Karmen writes that "many people, including some counselors and family therapists, believed that a high proportion of beatings were unconsciously precipitated or even intentionally provoked."

While battered women's advocates were attempting to replace a "victim-blaming" outlook with a "victim-defending" one, some of the same researchers who had already broken new ground in their exploration of child abuse began to address the issue of wife battering from a sociological perspective. These researchers' impersonal scientific approach lent an air of seriousness to a subject that had previously been dismissed by reactionaries. Domestic violence was suddenly the subject of scholarly journals and national academic conferences.

Data on wife abuse mounted and public awareness of the issue grew during the 1970s and 1980s, until Congress passed the Violence Against Women Act (VAWA) in 1994. Similarly to CAPTA, the VAWA provides federal funds to states for police, prosecutors, and prevention services in cases involving domestic abuse. Many states now use these funds to finance victims' counseling programs or increased police enforcement of spousal abuse laws.

As public and academic acknowledgment of child abuse and wife battering has grown, other victims of family violence have been identified. The growing elderly population is increasingly included in family violence research. Many researchers are finding that men as well as women are victims of spousal abuse. And recent family violence research has expanded to address abusive behavior between siblings and in gay and lesbian relationships.

The different forms that family violence can take will be explored in this book's first chapter: "Who Are the Victims of Family Violence?" Other chapters include "Is the Prevalence of Family Violence Exaggerated?" "What Are the Causes of Family Violence?" and "How Can Family Violence Be Reduced?" It is hoped that the viewpoints in *Family Violence: Current Controversies* will help readers understand the ongoing debates surrounding this serious social problem.

Chapter 1

Who Are the Victims of Family Violence?

Chapter Preface

Delia was a very young woman when she got married. Although she and her husband eventually had five children together, all was not well in the family. Delia's husband not only abused her but also assaulted and terrorized the children. He would laugh as he played Russian Roulette with a loaded gun.

A devout Roman Catholic, Delia sought help and advice from her family, but was told she needed to stay with her husband because they were married. Despite running away, asking for help, and even obtaining a protection order, Delia could not escape her violent spouse. She ultimately killed her husband and served several years in prison for the crime.

Delia's story, recounted by director M. Garguilo in her video *Broken Vows: Religious Perspectives on Domestic Violence*, is not atypical. Alan Kemp, author of *Abuse in the Family: An Introduction*, writes that many battered women endure years of mistreatment before finally retaliating against an abusive partner.

Researchers A. Browne and K.R. Williams found in separate studies that when women perpetrate violence, it is commonly in response to a protracted cycle of victimization. Sociologist A. Goetting reviewed 84 police reports of cases involving attempted spousal homicide and also determined that when women kill, they are most likely to do so for reasons of self-protection. She found that men, however, are more prone to kill for "offensive" reasons. Men are also more likely to kill their children as well as their wives.

Although the psychological motivations may differ for men and women who commit domestic violence, social scientist R. Gelles cites studies indicating that women are equally likely to use violence against their husbands. In his 1995 report to the American Medical Association, Gelles documents the results of the 1975 and 1985 National Family Violence Surveys, both of which indicated that women are as likely as their husbands (and perhaps even slightly more so) to initiate serious violence in a relationship.

Gelles also warns, however, that violence perpetrated by men may have a greater impact, and other research seems to bear him out. In M. Strauss's 1993 review of the second National Family Violence Survey, he found that men were six times more likely to inflict serious injuries on their wives than wives were on their husbands.

Although an important factor, gender is but one of the variables at play in the occurrence of violence in the family. As the following chapter shows, traditional attitudes about who makes up a family and what constitutes violence continue to be expanded by researchers investigating the phenomenon of family violence.

Women Are Victims of Family Violence

by Ann Jones

About the author: *Author Ann Jones has conducted extensive interviews of female victims of domestic violence. This viewpoint is excerpted from her book* Next Time She'll Be Dead: Battering and How to Stop It.

"Domestic violence" is the leading cause of injury to women in the United States. According to the National Clearinghouse on Domestic Violence, men batter three or four million women a year. According to the National Centers for Disease Control, more women are treated in emergency rooms for battering injuries than for (nonmarital) rapes, muggings, and traffic accidents *combined*. Untold numbers of women suffer permanent injuries—brain damage, blindness, deafness, speech loss through laryngeal damage, disfigurement and mutilation, damage to or loss of internal organs, paralysis, sterility, and so on. Countless pregnant women miscarry as a result of beatings, and countless birth defects and abnormalities can be attributed to battery of the mother during pregnancy. So many battered women have been infected with HIV by batterers who force them into unprotected sex, in some cases deliberately to prevent their having sex with other men, that the National Centers for Disease Control have identified a direct link between battering and the spread of HIV and AIDS among women. And every day at least four women die violently at the hands of men who profess to love them.

The Effects of Battering

After they escape, battered women may be saddled for years with a load of complicated problems ranging from anxiety, shame, and despair to flashbacks and suicidal ideation. These aftershocks are the symptoms of post-traumatic stress disorder, a psychological syndrome seen also in survivors of rape and incest and in veterans of wartime combat. Judith Lewis Herman notes the "horrifying" implications of this shared symptomatology: "There is war between the sexes. Rape victims, battered women, and sexually abused children are its casualties." Herman calls post-traumatic stress disorder the "combat neurosis of the sex war." In her view, however, the diagnosis of post-traumatic stress disorder, as it is now defined, doesn't begin to cover the problems of battered women. The current diagnostic criteria are drawn from survivors of discrete and limited traumatic events, such as combat, disaster, and rape; but the prolonged and repeated trauma of battery, like prolonged sexual abuse of a child, is of a different magnitude and resonance. Herman proposes to add to the clinical lexicon a new name for the aftermath of prolonged trauma: "complex post-traumatic stress disorder."

Violence Is More Than a Physical Act

But battering is something more than the sum of all these afflictions. "Emerge," a Boston counseling program for men who batter, uses this working definition: violence is "any act that causes the victim to do something she does not want to do, prevents her from doing something she wants to do, or causes her to be afraid." And they note that "violence *need not involve physical contact with the victim,* since intimidating acts like punching walls, verbal threats, and psychological abuse can achieve the same results." Psychological abuse, which they define as "behavior that directly undermines . . . self-determination or self-esteem," becomes "particularly powerful" when mixed with physical violence. Behavior you might not think of as "violence," behavior you might think of merely as getting things off your chest—such as "yelling, swearing, sulking, and angry accusations"—is violence if it coerces or frightens another person. And the likelihood of its doing just that increases exponentially when it's "'reinforced' by periodic or even occasional [physical] violence."

> *"There is a war between the sexes. Rape victims, battered women, and sexually abused children are its casualties."*

It's vital to understand that battering is *not* a series of isolated blow-ups. It is a *process of deliberate intimidation intended to coerce the victim to do the will of the victimizer.* The batterer is not just losing his temper, not just suffering from stress, not just manifesting "insecurity" or a spontaneous reaction "provoked" by something the victim did or (as psychologists put it) "a deficit of interpersonal skills" or an "inhibition in anger control mechanisms." These are *excuses* for violence, popular even among therapists who work with batterers; yet we all know aggrieved, insecure, stressed-out people with meager interpersonal skills who lose their temper *without* becoming violent. We assume, then, that the grievances of the violent man must be worse, and that under extreme stress he has spun out of control. He looks it, and that's what he says: "I wasn't myself." "I was drunk." "I went bananas." "I lost it." "I went out of my mind." It's lines like these that provide a public excuse and deceive a battered woman into giving one more chance to the so-called *real,* nonviolent man underneath. But in fact that violence *is* himself, perfectly *in* control and *exercising* control.

Batterers Control Their Victims

Counselor David Adams of Emerge observes that how a man deals with stress, or feelings, or conflict depends upon whom he's dealing *with,* and particularly upon the sex and status of that other person. Batterers can be perfectly agreeable, straightforward, or conciliatory to police officers, bosses, neighbors, co-workers, or friends when they think it's in their best interests. If they don't use those "interpersonal skills" with their wives, it's because they think it's *not* in their best interests; they *choose* not to. As Adams puts it: "The violent husband's selectively abusive behavior indicates an established set of *control skills.*" No, the

> *"The violent husband's selectively abusive behavior indicates an established set of control skills."*

violent man is not out of control. He is a man at work on his own agenda, which is to train "his" woman to be what he wants her to be, and only what he wants her to be, all the time.

Those control skills have been well documented, and they resemble nothing so much as the tactics used by Nazi guards to control prisoners in the death camps, and by Chinese thought-reformers to brainwash American P.O.W.'s in Korea. . . .

You may not have thought about battering in this way before. Many people haven't. But it's this unspoken agenda of the batterer that makes it so difficult for a woman to think of what to do, or even to grasp what's going on. (Battered women commonly report great confusion and the fear that they must be going crazy.) Most women, wanting to make the relationship work, will try to figure out rationally how they can change their own behavior to help the batterer stop battering. He says he hit her because the house is a mess or she shouldn't go out in shorts or she ought to stay home? She'll clean the house and dress "modestly" and quit her job—anything to stop the abuse. But because the abuser intends a coercion far more profound than any immediate "reason" for any particular incident, whatever the woman does—short of surrendering utterly to his will—must fail.

Batterers Devalue Their Victims

It's doubtful any living woman could meet the rigid specifications of the batterer. Emerge counselors observe that even when batterers purport to be "working" on their "relationship," they are intent upon *devaluing* their partner rather than *understanding* her. Typically, they denigrate what women say with comments like "She went on and on about nothing" or "She was in a bitchy mood," but when pressed by counselors, David Adams says, "men cannot recall their wives' actual words or specific complaints." Many counselors observe that what a batterer calls "nagging" is a woman's repetition of what she *knows* he hasn't heard. Counseling batterers in Duluth, Minnesota, Ellen Pence noticed that men rarely call the women they abuse by *name,* presumably because they don't see women as persons in their own right. In one men's group session, she counted ninety-seven references to wives and girlfriends, many of them obscene, before a man mentioned his wife by name. When Pence insisted they use names, many men "could hardly spit it out." Pence points out that many women still lose their last name at marriage; marry a controlling man, she says, and "Your front name goes too." Then the batterer tries to pummel this "nonentity" into the "person" he wants: the perfect wife.

Coercive Tactics Are Subtle

It's important to notice that . . . [the batterer's] . . . methods of coercion . . . take effect more or less "naturally" when a woman "falls in love." (The more she follows the prescribed formula of soap operas and romance novels, the farther she falls.) She spends less time with friends and focuses her attention on her new lover. He in turn "provides indulgences." And in the early giddy days of a relationship, she may enjoy trying to meet, even to anticipate, his trivial demands. If she's in love with a man (or woman) who feels the same and who respects her life, she may be on the way to a fine relationship. But if she has fallen for a controlling, potentially violent man, she is in serious trouble, because our traditional notions of romantic love have already given him a head start on coercion.

It's important to notice, too, that . . . thoroughgoing coercion—total destruction of the will—can be accomplished *without physical violence,* although batterers commonly add all sorts of bodily assault and sexual sadism, interspersed with those occasional "indulgences" and periods of professed remorse and reformation. Those seductive periods of male contrition, so convincing that psychologists label them "honeymoon phases" of the "cycle of violence" and women mistake them for love, are not respites from battering, as they appear, but part of the coercive process, pressuring women to forgive and forget, to minimize and deny, to *submit,* and thus to appear complicitous: they *are* battering."

> *"When batterers purport to be 'working' on their 'relationships,' they are intent upon devaluing their partner rather than understanding her."*

Violence May Become Extreme

In the extreme, physical violence passes over into torture: sleep deprivation, burns, electric shock, bondage, semi -starvation, choking, near-drowning, exposure, mutilation, rape, forcible rape with objects or animals, and so on. Amnesty International defines torture as "the systematic and deliberate infliction of acute pain in any form by one person on another, or on a third person, in order to accomplish the purpose of the former against the will of the latter." The organization says that "regardless of the context in which it is used, torture is outlawed under the common law of mankind" and "may properly be considered to be a crime against humanity." Yet the terrible stories told by war prisoners and hostages delivered from bondage and torture can be matched by the stories of battered women. The batterer may be less skilled than the professional thought-reformer, but he acts to the same purpose: to control the life of another. And even perfect control may not be enough for him. Judith Lewis Herman explains that the dominating man needs the victim's "affirmation" to justify his crimes. In situations of political captivity and domestic captivity alike, the captor is rarely satisfied with simple compliance. "Thus," Herman writes, "he relentlessly demands from his victim professions of respect, gratitude, or even love. His ultimate goal appears to be the creation of a willing victim."

> *"Thoroughgoing coercion— total destruction of the will— can be accomplished* **without physical violence.***"*

The Psychology of the Victim

It is equally vital to understand that women are battered *because they will not give in*. One survivor who now counsels abused women put it this way: "Most of the battered women I meet are really strong women, and that's why they get beat—because they don't take no shit. And that's why I got beat—because I wouldn't act like he wanted me to act, talk like he wanted me to talk, be who he wanted me to be." As I've said, the FBI reports that a woman is beaten in the United States every ten seconds or so, but we can better understand what's going on by thinking of it this way: every ten seconds a woman *resists*.

Her concerns are complex. Like most women, battered or not, she probably places a higher value on human connections and the compromises necessary to preserve them than do most men; and despite her shock and anger, there is no one who has greater compassion for the batterer, at least at first, than the battered woman herself. But she also values herself. Under threat of violence, a woman may give up bits and pieces of herself: her preferences, her opinions, her voice, her friends, her job, her freedom of movement, her sexual autonomy. She may learn to lie, or at least to keep the truth to herself. She may learn to say the sex was good when it wasn't, or that she's sorry when she's not. Unable ever to give the "right" answer, she may retreat into silence. It's often easy to mistake her apparent passivity for submission, masochism, complicity. But she does not give in. Uncle Remus and Br'er Rabbit, experts on outwitting violent oppression, called it "laying low." A battered woman lies low while she tries first to make sense of her situation, then to change it, and finally to get out.

Battered Women Eventually Get Out

In the long run, battering a woman to control her is almost certain to fail, for battered women *leave*. It is not too much to say that from the first moment a man abuses her, a woman begins, in some sense, to leave—emotionally, spiritually, physically. Shocked at first, she may try to stop the violence by trying to become "a better person," but she ends by trying to be in another place. She may embezzle from the grocery money for months, placating the batterer all the while she squirrels away the price of a ticket to freedom. Abused women describe this process of going underground within themselves, hiding out inside, lying low until they can emerge, like some moth shedding caterpillar skin, becoming themselves. Escapees say: "Now I'm *myself* again."

When it comes to getting out, women are enormously ingenious, resourceful, and brave. They have to be because it's at this point—when "his woman" escapes—that the abuser is most dangerous. Absolutely dependent upon her submission for his own sense of power and control, he can not bear to lose her. In many cases, that false sense of power is the only identity a man has; to lose "his woman" is to lose himself. Thus, he is far more likely to kill her (and perhaps himself as well) as she tries to leave or *after she has left*, than if she stays with him. ("If I can't have you, nobody can," he says.)

Battered women know this, and they leave anyway. One formerly battered woman explained to talk show host Sally Jessy Raphael: "It takes a lot of maneuvering, a lot of mental exercise, to get out." At a speak-out for formerly battered women in Seattle, a woman who had been afraid for her life described her escape into hiding: she booked an early morning flight to a distant city, then asked her husband for permission to go regularly to early mass to pray for God's guidance in "being a better wife." "On Monday I went to mass," she said. "On Tuesday I went to mass. On Wednesday I went to mass. On Thursday I went to the airport." Another woman told me how she ejected a battering husband who refused to leave *her* house. "He's a boxer," she explained, "and he had closed in my garage as a workout room. What I did, while he was at work one day, was cut this giant hole in the garage door with a huge power saw, and I backed a truck up to the hole, and I took all his boxing training things and all his clothes and personal stuff and anything I thought he might want, and I put it on the truck, took it to his mother's house, dumped it in the yard, and said, 'Enough is enough.' Since then I'm on my third restraining order."

> **"Under threat of violence, a woman may give up bits and pieces of herself."**

Battering Reinforces Patterns of Male Dominance

In the short run though, battering *works*. It may be mean and cowardly and cruel and criminal and an evolutionary throwback, but for the batterer's immediate gratification, it works fine. Just as many parents use physical force, or the threat of it, to make children "behave," many men know that there's nothing like a good pow in the kisser, or the threat of it, to keep the little lady in line.

Chapter 1

Individual men beat individual women to make those women do what they want. And the widespread practice of wife beating intimidates all women and reinforces our society's habitual pattern of male dominance. A little muscle gets a guy a little sex, a little peace and quiet, a little attention, another drink, and in the great cosmic scheme of things, it helps keep a man's world a man's world. What could be more efficient?

Men Are Victims of Family Violence

by Nancy Updike

About the author: *Nancy Updike is a producer for Public Radio International and WBEZ-Chicago's "This American Life."*

A surprising fact has turned up in the grimly familiar world of domestic violence: Women report using violence in their relationships more often than men. This is not a crack by some antifeminist cad; the information . . . is contained in a . . . Justice Department . . . report summarizing the results of in-depth, face-to-face interviews with a representative sample of 860 men and women whom researchers have been following since birth. Conducted in New Zealand by Terrie Moffitt, a University of Wisconsin psychology professor, the study supports data published in 1980 indicating that wives hit their husbands at least as often as husbands hit their wives.

The Study of Domestic Violence Broadens

When the 1980 study was released, it was so controversial that some of the researchers received death threats. Advocates for battered women were outraged because the data seemed to suggest that the risk of injury from domestic violence is as high for men as it is for women, which isn't true. Whether or not women are violent themselves, they are much more likely to be severely injured or killed by domestic violence, so activists dismissed the findings as meaningless.

But Moffitt's research emerges in a very different context—namely, that of a movement that is older, wiser, and ready to begin making sense of uncomfortable truths. Twenty years ago, "domestic violence" meant men hitting women. Period. That was the only way to understand it or to talk about it. But today, after decades of research and activism predicated on that assumption, the number of women killed each year in domestic violence incidents remains distressingly high: a sobering 1,326 in 1996, compared with 1,600 two decades earlier. In light of the persistence of domestic violence, researchers are beginning to consider a broader range of data, including the possible significance of women's violence. This willingness to pay attention to what was once considered reactionary nonsense signals a fundamental conceptual shift in how domestic violence is being studied.

Statistics Are Difficult to Interpret

Violence in the home has never been easy to research. Even the way we measure it reflects the kind of murky data that has plagued the field. For instance, one could argue that the number of fatalities resulting from domestic violence is not the best measure of the problem, as not all acts of brutality end in death. It is, however, one of the few reliable statistics in a field where concrete numbers are difficult to come by. Many nonlethal domestic violence incidents go unreported or are categorized as something else—aggravated assault, simple assault—when they are reported. But another reason we haven't been able to effectively measure domestic violence is that we don't understand it, and, because we don't understand it, we haven't been able to stop it. Money and ideology are at the heart of the problem.

For years, domestic violence research was underfunded and conducted piecemeal, sometimes by researchers with more zeal for the cause of battered women than training in research methodology. The results were often ideology-driven "statistics," such as the notorious (and false) claim that more men beat their wives on Super Bowl Sunday, which dramatized the cause of domestic violence victims but further confused an already intricate issue. In 1994, Congress asked the National Research Council, an independent Washington, D.C., think tank, to evaluate the state of knowledge about domestic abuse. The NRC report concluded that "this field of research is characterized by the absence of clear conceptual models, large-scale databases, longitudinal research, and reliable instrumentation."

Changing Perspectives

Moffitt is part of a new wave of domestic violence researchers who are bringing expertise from other areas of study, and her work is symbolic of the way scientists are changing their conception of the roots of domestic violence.

"[She] is taking domestic violence out of its standard intellectual confines and putting it into a much larger context, that of violence in general," says Daniel Nagin, a crime researcher and the Theresa and H. John Heinz III

> *"Twenty years ago, 'domestic violence' meant men hitting women. Period."*

Professor of Public Policy at Carnegie Mellon University.

Moffitt is a developmental psychologist who has spent most of her career studying juvenile delinquency, which was the original focus of her research. She started interviewing her subjects about violence in their relationships after 20 years of research into other seemingly unrelated aspects of their lives: sex and drug-use habits, criminal activities, social networks and family ties, and signs of mental illness.

"I had looked at other studies of juvenile delinquency," Moffitt says, "and saw that people in their 20s were dropping out of street crime, and I wondered, 'Are all of these miraculous recoveries where they're just reforming and giving up crime? Or are they getting out of their parents' home and moving in with a girlfriend and finding victims who are more easily accessible?' So I decided we'd better not just ask them about street violence, but also about violence within the home, with a partner."

New Study Results

What she found was that the women in her study who were in violent relationships were more like their partners, in many ways, than they were like the other women in the study. Both the victims and the aggressors in violent relationships, Moffitt found, were more likely to be unemployed and less educated than couples in nonviolent relationships. Moffitt also found that "female perpetrators of partner violence differed from nonviolent women with respect to factors that could not be solely the result of being in a violent relationship." Her research disputes a long-held belief about the nature of domestic violence: If a woman hits, it's only in response to her partner's attacks. The

"For years, domestic violence research was underfunded and conducted piecemeal."

study suggests that some women may simply be prone to violence—by nature or circumstance—just as some men may be.

Moffitt's findings don't change the fact that women are much more at risk in domestic violence, but they do suggest new ways to search for the origins of violence in the home. And once we know which early experiences can lead to domestic violence, we can start to find ways to intervene before the problem begins.

Preconceptions Cloud the Issue

Prevention is a controversial goal, however, because it often calls for changes in the behavior of the victim as well as the batterer, and for decades activists have been promoting the seemingly opposite view. And even though it is possible to talk about prevention without blaming victims or excusing abusers, the issue is a minefield of preconceived ideas about gender, violence, and relationships, and new approaches may seem too scary to contemplate.

In domestic violence research, it seems, the meaning of any new data is predetermined by ideological agendas set a long time ago, and the fear that new information can be misinterpreted can lead to a rejection of the information itself. In preparing this column, I called a well-known women's research organization and asked scientists there about new FBI statistics indicating a substantial recent increase in violent crime committed by girls ages 12 to 18. The media contact told me the organization had decided not to collect any information about those statistics and that it didn't think it was a fruitful area of research, because girls are still much more likely to be victims of violence than perpetrators.

Further Research Is Needed

It's impossible to know yet whether such numbers are useful, whether they're a statistical blip or a trend, or whether the girls committing violent crimes now are more likely to end up in violent relationships. But to ignore them on principle—as activists and researchers ignored the data about women's violence years ago—is to give up on determining the roots of violence, which seem to be much more complicated than whether a person is born with a Y chromosome.

"[Moffitt's] research disputes a long-held belief about the nature of domestic violence: If a woman hits, it's only in response to her partner's attacks."

What's clear is that women's and girls' violence is not meaningless, either for researchers or for the women themselves. It turns out that teenage girls who commit violent crimes "are two times more likely than juvenile male offenders to become victims themselves in the course of the offending incident," according to an FBI report. I'd like to hear more about that, please, not less. Moffitt's findings about women's violence and the FBI statistics are invitations to further research—not in spite of the fact that so many women are being beaten and killed every year, but because of it.

Children Are Victims of Many Forms of Abuse

by George A. Gellert

About the author: *George A. Gellert is a physician specializing in epidemiology, public health, and child abuse. He is the author of* Confronting Violence: Answers to Questions About the Epidemic Destroying America's Homes and Communities.

Child abuse is a general term and includes physical abuse, psychological or emotional abuse, sexual abuse, assault or exploitation, and neglect. Child maltreatment is a less specific term that is often used to describe child abuse. The common theme running through all of these forms of abuse is the failure of a caretaker to provide responsible care for a child. The mandatory reporting systems for child abuse in many jurisdictions actually limit abuse to only acts committed by family household members or other caretakers. Child abuse does not always include the actions of strangers or acquaintances of the child. There is no standard definition of child abuse across the United States; each state has created its own legal definition. Commonly, the definitions include harm or a threat of harm to a child's health and welfare by the person responsible for the child. The physical or mental injury is inflicted in a nonaccidental manner.

Types of Child Abuse

Neglect is believed to be the most common of the four types of child abuse and can be the most life-threatening to the child. Features of neglect include the failure of a caretaker to provide basic shelter, medical and dental care, supervision, or emotional support to a child. Failure to provide adequate nutrition, hygienic care, and education may also occur with child neglect. Physical child abuse involves not only inflicting injury to a child through excessive force, but also forcing a child to engage in physically harmful activities.

Child sexual abuse is usually defined as any sexual contact between a child and an adult and, if there is a sufficient age difference, between juveniles. This definition is quite wide-ranging, and may include not only a father who has in-

Excerpted from George A. Gellert, *Confronting Violence: Answers to Questions About the Epidemic Destroying America's Homes and Communities*. Reprinted by permission of the author.

cestuous sexual intercourse with his daughter, but an individual who exposes himself sexually in front of a child. Most forms of sexual abuse fall between these two extreme forms. The major categories of child sexual abuse include incest, pedophilia (literally, "the love of children," often expressed as fondling, but which includes penetration), exhibitionism, molestation, statutory rape and rape, child prostitution, and child pornography. . . .

Emotional Abuse

Emotional abuse involves coercive, demeaning, or very distant behavior by a parent or other caretaker that interferes with a child's normal psychological or social development. Emotional abuse [also] involves acts, or the failure to act, on the part of parents and other care-givers that may cause serious emotional, cognitive, or behavioral problems in a child. These acts, or inattention and indifference to emotional needs, can very negatively impact upon the well-being of a child.

Emotional abuse can involve several different kinds of traumatic acts or attitudes on the part of parents and care-givers, including rejecting a child's worth or the legitimacy of the child's needs, isolating a child from usual social experiences, and making the child feel alone in the world. Imposing unreasonable parental demands on a child, or creating unrealistically high objectives or standards of achievement can be emotionally abusive. Terrorizing the child by frightening, bullying, and verbally assaulting him or her is emotionally abusive. In addition, ignoring a child's need for developmental and emotional stimulation can compromise that individual's growth to healthy adulthood. Compelling children to engage in destructive and antisocial behaviors [also] has a corrupting impact that makes the child unfit for normal social experiences and is another form of emotional abuse. The frequency of emotional abuse is not well measured. The different forms of child abuse may occur together, and the child who is physically or sexually abused or neglected is, almost by definition, harmed psychologically.

> *"The common theme running through all . . . forms of abuse is the failure of a caretaker to provide responsible care for a child."*

When Was Child Abuse First Recognized?

While child abuse was recognized over one hundred years ago for the first time, widespread action to prevent it and treat abuse victims has been much slower in coming. The first victim of child abuse was recorded in the United States in 1874. Within a year, New York State had passed the first child abuse law in the nation, and the Society for the Prevention of Cruelty to Children was founded. Thus social recognition of child abuse long preceded substantial professional interest and effort to manage the problem.

Almost 100 years later, the medical profession first offered a term to describe child abuse. Dr. C. Henry Kempe and colleagues described "the battered child syndrome" in a 1962 medical journal article. The article had a profound effect and generated many newspaper reports and magazine articles, and soon the topic of child abuse was an occasional theme on television medical programs. However, it was not until the late sixties that all U.S. states had child abuse reporting laws in place. In 1974, legislation required states to report all forms of maltreatment, including neglect and sexual abuse, in addition to physical abuse. However, even today many states continue to have shortages in staff and resources in the area of child protection services, and there is a need for improved collaboration and cooperation between health, social service, law enforcement, and criminal justice agencies responding to the child abuse problem.

> *"The first victim of child abuse was recorded in the United States in 1874."*

How Common Is Child Abuse?

Every thirteen seconds an American child is reported as abused or neglected. Each day almost 2,000 children become victims of abuse or neglect. Estimates of the national incidence and prevalence of child abuse and neglect suggest that at least twenty-five children of every 1,000 nationwide annually experience abuse or neglect. This represents between 2 and 3 percent of the total population under the age of eighteen years. The most frequent type of abuse is thought to be physical. While it is almost impossible to accurately estimate the extent of emotional abuse, sexual abuse occurs less frequently. In 1986, 300,000 children were estimated to have been physically abused and 700,000 were neglected. Approximately two-thirds of the annual reports concern neglect of children. It is estimated that 160,000 children suffered serious or life-threatening injuries as a result of child abuse. Emotional and learning problems occur in almost all victims.

Reported cases of child abuse have been mounting for several years. Over the course of the eighties, the number of child abuse reports increased by almost 200 percent. In 1991, state child protective service agencies received reports of 1.8 million instances of abuse and neglect involving 2.7 million children. It is unclear from this, however, that the actual occurrence of child abuse has been increasing. Reporting can increase despite a stable incidence as social awareness is heightened by greater coverage of child abuse in the media. In 1993, over 1,300 abuse-related deaths were reported. Remarkably, of these, 42 percent of the families involved were previously reported for child abuse. Research has suggested that between five and eleven of every 100,000 children four years old and younger are killed by abuse and neglect. A 1996 report from the United States Department of Health and Human Services stated that between 1986 and 1993, the number of abused and neglected children doubled to more than 2.8 million.

Homicide and Sexual Abuse

Child homicide is among the top five causes of death in childhood and accounts for approximately 5 percent of all deaths among individuals below the age of eighteen. The majority of infant victims are killed by parents and relatives, while older children are more frequently killed by strangers, acquaintances, or perpetrators who remain unidentified. An estimated 1,200–2,000 childhood deaths occur each year as a result of maltreatment, and of these, over 80 percent are under the age of 5 and 40 percent are in the first year of life. Because deaths by abuse and neglect may be confused with natural causes that can occur at the same time as and perhaps as a result of abuse (such as pneumonia or malnutrition), there are those who believe that the number of children dying from maltreatment in the U.S. may be as high as 5,000 per year.

Sexual abuse of children is the form of abuse that is growing most rapidly in terms of reporting. Approximately one-sixth of all maltreatment reports involve sexual assault, and 150,000 to 200,000 sexual abuse reports are filed annually in the United States. . . .

Reporting Child Abuse

Several factors can influence whether a case of child abuse is reported or not. The socioeconomic class and race of the perpetrator partly determine whether a particular incident of abuse is reported. Abuse occurring in black and Latino families is more likely to be reported than that in white families, and those with the lowest incomes have higher rates of reporting than families earning $25,000 or more per year. Child abuse, and particularly fatal child abuse, have challenged the stereotype that violence in the home affects only poor or otherwise disadvantaged families. Child abuse occurs at all levels of society. Neglect and physical abuse increase in frequency with greater poverty, but may be found in the highest income homes as well. The frequency of sexual abuse is fairly constant across all income groups. There appears to be some indifference to child abuse in more affluent and majority-race (white) homes, which might suggest that these families are less at risk for abuse of children. Research has indicated that this is not the case, and that these differences are due to a bias in reporting.

In any case, the frequency of reporting of abuse to protective services is greatly below the actual level of violence against children. Studies have shown that perhaps as low as one in seven cases of severe physical abuse were reported. One in ten parents have admitted to using severe violence with their children, including hitting, kicking, beating, threatening, or using knives or firearms.

> *"Over the course of the eighties, the number of child abuse reports increased by almost 200 percent."*

One-fifth to one-third of all women report experiencing some form of child sexual abuse during their childhood, most often perpetrated by an adult male. In one study, 27 percent of women and 16 percent of men reported a history of child sexual abuse. This would suggest that up to 38 million adult Americans were sexually abused as children. The majority of the perpetrators were known to the victims, and one-third were family members. In less than one-third of all instances was the perpetrator a stranger. Some experts believe that perhaps one-fifth of all Americans have been the victims of child sexual abuse. One-third of victims never report the abuse and live with the history of abuse as a secret throughout their adulthood.

The Signs of Abuse

Children who are the victims of child abuse may have a wide variety of physical signs and symptoms, or in some circumstances very few. These can range from broken bones, bruises, lacerations, and serious injuries that require hospitalization to very subtle manifestations. Often there are multiple wounds in different stages of healing. There may also be wounds in the shape or pattern of a recognizable object. The trauma apparent on the child's body is often inconsistent with the explanation given by the parent or care-giver. A possible sign of abuse is that the parent or care-giver's story changes with each retelling or involves an incident that was unwitnessed, such as a fall or hot water scalding of a child in a bath while the caretaker "stepped out for a moment."

> *"One in ten parents have admitted to using severe violence with their children, including hitting, kicking, beating, threatening, or using knives or firearms."*

These features may occur in combination with a failure of the child to grow and evidence of chronic malnutrition. The child may have fallen off the normal curve of growth by weight and height and fall near the lowest 5–10 percent of his or her age group. There may be unexplained injuries to the teeth or mouth. A child may sometimes appear with two black eyes and the parent reporting that there was only a single accidental blow or fall. In some instances children may have burns or evidence of poisoning. In child sexual abuse, bruising and tearing of the genitals or the anus may be evident, and the child may complain of pain in these areas.

A Variety of Indicators

Unusual patterns of bruising may also be apparent in children who have been abused. For example, a bruise around the sides of the mouth and continuing along the cheeks may have been left by a gag. Bruises of various colors indicate that they are in different stages of healing, and this suggests a long-term history of injury not consistent with a single fall or other accident as claimed by a parent. Blistering and swelling of the skin may occur around the wrist of a child who has been tied up, and over the long-term, this may cause lasting changes to the pigment of the skin. Bite marks may be apparent on a child as well. Loop or cord marks on the back and buttocks may indicate that a child has been whipped with an electrical cord or a belt. Several fingers may leave their impression as half-inch parallel columns on the face of a child who has been slapped repeatedly. Children who have been immersed in hot water will have typical burn patterns that are sharply segmented according to what parts of the body did or did not enter the water. Scalding from splashing hot liquids can appear anywhere on the body but is more common on the torso. Cigarette and cigar burns may be observed. Hair-pulling is a common form of abuse and may result in a traumatic area of baldness.

Broken ribs in the absence of major trauma such as a car crash are suspicious, as are fractures of the long bones of the legs or arms. Similarly, skull fractures after what are reported as short distance falls may have actually occurred as a result of child abuse. Other injuries, such as to the organs of the abdomen and chest, may only be detected by a physician or other trained health professional.

Psychological Effects

The psychological effects of abuse may be profound. Children who are the victims of abuse may be socially and emotionally withdrawn. They may suffer from acute anxiety attacks and nightmares. Bed-wetting, thumbsucking, and other forms of regressive behavior may be evident. They may have trouble forming social relationships with adults and other children in the home environment or at school and may become antisocial. Often these children will begin to deteriorate in school performance and have decreased interest in recreational activities. Eating disorders, hypochondria, nightmares, anxiety, apathy, and destructive and self-destructive behaviors may occur in physically or emotionally abused children. Neglect may be evident in a child with poor personal hygiene or clothing that is inappropriate to the weather. Emotional extremes among victims are common, with excessive or no crying, behavior that is very aggressive or passive, highly fearful or fearless.

> *"The trauma apparent on the child's body is often inconsistent with the explanation given by the parent or care-giver."*

A child who has been victimized by abuse will frequently not be forthcoming in reporting abuse. Children often experience acute shame or fear of reprisal from the abuser. Abusers may tell the children that if they report the abuse they will be killed, otherwise harmed, or that the child's family may be harmed by the abuser.

The Elderly Are Vulnerable to Abuse

by Sabine Krummel

About the author: Sabine Krummel is the director of family services at ARC Otsego, in Oneonta, New York. She has received specialized training in medical family therapy, experiential family therapy, and working with the elderly.

In the past three years things have gotten steadily worse. My daughter locked me in the garage and left me there. . . . Whenever I tried to cook a meal, she would appear and turn off the gas and remove the grills so that the only way I could cook was to hold the pan over the fire. . . . My daughter's treatment of me kept getting worse. Always hurting me physically and mentally, kicking me, pushing me, grappling with me. . . . She is a well-educated person.

—voice of an elderly woman

The thing that bothered me most about my mother-in-law was constant demands—unreasonable demands—towards the end she really got bad. She wouldn't let me sleep. Ten to fifteen minutes, then she would call me again. All day and night she would do this, all day and night. . . .

—voice of a caregiver

Victimization of the elderly by their adult children has only recently been acknowledged as a significant social problem. Within the last two decades the consensus on the prevalence of elder abuse has been estimated to range from 3 to 5% of all elders. This suggests that elder abuse is almost, if not equally, as pervasive as child abuse in our society. In addition, it is all too readily assumed that elder abuse occurs primarily in nursing homes rather than at the hands of loved ones. This belief is unfounded; at any given time, fewer than 5% of individuals over the age of 60 live in institutions.

Elder Abuse Cannot Be Ignored

What is currently a significant social problem may escalate into an unmanageable quandary if ignored. Currently industrialized countries are experiencing an elder "boom" because of rapid advances in medical interventions. The fastest growing age group is 85 years and over. Approximately 33% of the U.S. population in 2020 will be 55 years old or older. It is estimated that within 10 to 20 years, close to 50% of all deaths will occur after the age of 80. Obviously, the future implications for the family are immense in terms of time, emotional support, and financial assistance required from the younger generation for the elderly.

In addition, the "younger generation" may no longer be so young, because parents in their eighties tend to have children in their sixties. Caretakers in their retirement years often express frustration, anger, and guilt regarding responsibility for their elderly parent. This frustration is verbalized by a 66-year-old daughter caring for her 86-year-old father.

> He has lived his life. I should have a chance to live mine. I worked forty-five years of my life and I would like to have a little time to live before I die. There are times when it crops up . . . when I feel so guilty about feeling like I do that I just think I must be no good to anybody. . . . There are times when I think, if I could die and get out of the whole stinking mess . . . without having to live with it day in and day out.

Gender Differences Affect Relationships

Besides the increased percentage of the elderly in our society, it becomes essential to incorporate the broader context of sex differences in both the caregivers and the elderly. Although the title "caregiver" portrays a sexless image, research indicates that a disproportionate number of elders are cared for by the women in our society. In general, single, divorced, or widowed daughters provide more care than do married daughters. Daughters tend not only to live closer to their parents, but also to feel more responsibility for their parents' well-being. Whereas sons provide financial support, daughters are more closely involved with daily caregiving for the elderly such as chores, meals, and emotional support. Paradoxically, married sons have a higher tendency to take in an elderly parent than single sons, which suggests that they rely on their wives to provide the major caregiving.

Similar to "caregiver," the word *elderly* does not identify any gender differences. Nevertheless, research has consistently indicated that women have a longer life expectancy than men. In 1979 for every 100 women over the age of 65, 68.4 men existed. This disproportion tends to increase with age. In addition, older women struggle not only with ageism, but

> *"Caretakers in their retirement years often express frustration, anger, and guilt regarding responsibility for their elderly parent."*

also with sexism. Older women are often portrayed as "hags" or "old bags" long before men receive equally slanderous remarks. Besides outer appearance, a large discrepancy exists between older men and women regarding the financial resources available to each. Whereas men tend to be able to rely on at least a limited pension, most women have no financial security in old age. As few as 2% of older women benefit from widows' survivor benefits following their husbands' deaths. Many women perceive their economic crisis as a personal failure rather than as a social and economic injustice within the social system.

Definition of Elder Abuse

When dealing with the abused elderly, the . . . first hurdle is to decide what exactly constitutes abuse. A workable definition describes *elder abuse* as physical injury or neglect, financial exploitation, mental torment, unreasonable confinement, or denial of services necessary for the maintenance of mental and physical health. Five categories provide a multifaceted criterion by which to identify elder abuse:

- *Physical abuse* refers to being beaten, slapped, bruised, cut, burned, physically restrained, or drugged by a caretaker. Multiple bruises at different stages of healing are a common indication of elder abuse.
- *Psychological abuse* refers to the instance of an elderly person being ridiculed, manipulated, treated as a child, frightened, humiliated, shamed, or called names. Although psychological abuse tends to be difficult to measure, it is consistently reported that it tends to cause even more distress and anguish than does physical abuse.

> *"Whereas men tend to be able to rely on at least a limited pension, most women have no financial security in old age."*

- *Financial abuse* refers to inappropriate and illegal exploitation of the elderly's resources. Indications of financial abuse include excessive and expensive "gifts," multiple withdrawals from a bank account over a short period of time, disappearance of valuable possessions, or illegally signed checks and documents.
- *Active neglect* involves the violation of rights of all citizens. These rights include freedom of speech, religion, and the rights to vote and assemble. Active neglect, therefore, includes withholding food, medicine, or bathroom assistance, as well as denying the elderly the right to open their own mail, attend the church of their choice, maintain contact with friends, or use the telephone.
- *Passive neglect* is defined as harm inflicted on the elderly because of inadequate knowledge of the changing needs of aging adults. Appropriate food intake and medical supervision are ignored and result in starvation, dehydration, and medical emergencies. The elderly person is often left alone for unreasonable time spans, isolated from stimulation, or altogether forgotten.

The majority of research on elder abuse identifies the victims as primarily white women who are widowed or single and over the age of 75. Many victims are physically or mentally impaired and are dependent on their caregivers.

Abusers of the elderly are described as primarily being adult sons, who suffer from some form of psychopathology and are dependent on their elderly parents. A more recent study has challenged these findings, suggesting that perpetrators of elder abuse are spouses in up to 60% of cases. This study also suggests that men are as likely to be abused by caregivers as women. Nevertheless, most studies agree that women suffer more severely from both physical and psychological abuse than men do. Elders who live with their perpetrators are at higher risk for abuse by their adult children than those living alone because of the greater opportunities for interaction.

"The majority of research on elder abuse identifies the victims as primarily white women who are widowed or single and over the age of 75."

Studies repeatedly suggest that abuse is present in all age groups, economic levels, and various ethnic groups among the elderly. Nevertheless, the limited research on African American families suggests that black elderly individuals experience far less abuse by their adult children than do white elders. It is speculated that the extended family network and strong cohesiveness within black families serve as a buffer to abuse. In addition, African American families often encourage their adult children to return to the home of their elderly mothers because of a strong matriarchal family structure. By contrast, elderly white persons tend to move into their children's home. Similar patterns are found in Latin American and native American families. Nevertheless, research on these three ethnic groups continues to be limited and more attention is needed in the future.

Gays and Lesbians Are Often Victims

by George Appleby and Jeane Anastas

About the authors: *George Appleby and Jeane Anastas began working together to address gay and lesbian issues in the early 1990s. They have given workshops together at professional conferences, and are coauthors of the book* Not Just a Passing Phase, *from which this viewpoint is excerpted.*

Violence against gay and lesbian people can be easily dismissed as a problem by many because it expresses widely held attitudes; similarly because gay and lesbian relationships are either invisible (these are just "roommates" or "friends" who got into a fight) or are seen as dysfunctional anyway, the problem of domestic violence in gay and lesbian relationships has long gone unrecognized. When it comes to domestic violence, however, the gay and lesbian communities themselves have also been slow to acknowledge the problem despite the fact that it is now suggested that domestic violence may be as common in gay and lesbian relationships as it is in heterosexual ones.

False Assumptions Impede Research

Research related to the nature of domestic violence in lesbian and gay relationships is thwarted by many false assumptions commonly accepted in gay and lesbian communities. Two of these assumptions are that domestic violence is only physical abuse and that any abuse perpetrated by a lesbian or gay man is not that dangerous or harmful because of the relatively equal size and strength of same-gender partners. Other myths and misconceptions have been identified as reasons why gay-on-gay domestic violence is most often not recognized or labeled as such. [As D. Island and P. Letellier state,]

> Only straight women get battered; gay men are never victims. Domestic violence is more common in straight relationships than in gay male relationships. Gay domestic violence is a "fight" and when two men fight it is a fair fight between equals. It is not really violence when two men fight; it is normal; it is boys being boys. Gay men's domestic violence is just a lovers' quarrel. The

batterer will always be bigger and stronger; the victim will always be smaller and weaker. Men who are abusive while under the influence of drugs or alcohol are not responsible for their actions. Gay men's domestic violence has increased as a result of the AIDS epidemic, alcoholism, and drug abuse. Gay men's domestic violence is sexual behavior, a version of sadomasochism; the victims actually like it. The law does not protect victims of gay men's domestic violence.

These myths keep the gay community as well as the community at large from taking responsibility and action. The myths also serve as powerful forces for keeping gay men and lesbians in abusive relationships. However, these myths and assumptions run counter to the empirical data gleaned from survivors and research participants.

Denial of the Problem

Another reason that the gay and lesbian community has resisted acknowledging the problem of domestic violence is because it is believed that widespread knowledge of this problem would add to already high levels of antigay discrimination. As Island and Letellier put it with respect to gay men:

> Gay men generally believe they are more affluent than their straight brothers, are better educated, are in better physical shape, and make a significant effort to lead a more enlightened lifestyle. But, if the gay community really did take its own domestic violence seriously, it would mean that gays themselves [would be required to give up a powerful defense mechanism, denial, and] would have to recognize that gay men truly are not only ordinary people but also have [their] proportionate share of violent individuals in their midst who bash other gay men in startlingly high numbers.

For the lesbian community, the issues are similar in that recognizing that lesbians are both victims and perpetrators constitutes an uncomfortable fact. Denial also serves to maintain the false assumption that only men are batterers and only women are victims. Men are supposed to be in control of their lives and therefore immune to victimization. A narrow definition of sexism does not allow for lesbian abusers. Finally, denial attempts to negate heterosexist assumptions that gay and lesbian relationships are inherently sick and seeks to reduce any further justification for de-

> *"Denial . . . serves to maintain the false assumption that only men are batterers and only women are victims."*

valuing gay and lesbian lives or for escalating violence and discrimination.

Unfortunately, however, lesbians and gay men can be and are battered or abused by a family member, roommate, lover, ex-spouse, or ex-lover. Anecdotal evidence suggests that some victims seek help and tell authorities the real reason they are doing so and some victims seek help without revealing the real reason. However, most victims don't tell anyone at all, and the authorities fail to ask if a reported assault is domestic violence. Nearly all batterers do not tell anyone and do not seek help voluntarily. This pattern is much like that seen in heterosexual domestic violence, although gay and lesbian people fear the heterosexism and homophobia of potential helpers along with all the other barriers to seeking assistance that all domestic abuse victims experience.

The Extent of the Problem

Although gay men's domestic violence is a newly recognized problem, it has existed since gay men began coupling and living together. What is new about it is that all over the country gay men are coming forward to seek help as victims of domestic violence. These estimated half million battered men, along with an equal number of perpetrators, face a gay community and a society in general that are ill-prepared to help them. [According to Island and Letellier,] it is estimated that "only substance abuse and AIDS adversely affect more gay men, making domestic violence the third largest health problem facing gay men today." The actual numbers are hard to come by because domestic violence is a taboo subject. For authorities to show interest by collecting data would mean that something should be done. Because sodomy is still a crime in many states and because gay-bashing is still widely ignored, there are many disincentives for reporting the problem, and legal intervention on behalf of battered gay men has little political capital.

Similarly, battering and other forms of physical violence in lesbian relationships is not a new phenomenon but a rather newly recognized one. Although the women's shelter movement is recently increasing its attention to serving women who are being abused in their relationships with other women, it is not clear that lesbian women feel comfortable seeking help in these settings, and it is only by reporting the problem or seeking help with it that the prevalence of the problem will become known. Isolation is often a major problem; as A.M. Waldron notes, "Often, because of a reluctance to identify as a lesbian, the battering lesbian partner is the only other lesbian with whom the battered lesbian has extensive contact." Nevertheless it has been estimated that 22 to 46 percent of all lesbians have been involved in a lesbian relationship in which physical violence occurred. Where there is acceptance that gay and lesbian domestic abuse exists, there is often the assumption that it affects only certain groups within the gay and lesbian community. Violent and abusive behavior are found in all segments of the gay and lesbian community, without regard for race, class, ethnicity, age, ability, education, politics, or religion. However, some subgroups within the community, such as gay men and lesbians of color, may find it even more difficult than others to identify sources of help that they can trust. The few studies of gay and lesbian domestic abuse that do exist concluded that neither the victim nor the perpetrator are easily identified. These misconceptions are often similar to those held about heterosexual abusive relationships. . . .

Many of the models for understanding and stopping domestic violence come from the battered women's movement and are applied to the gay and lesbian communities. Whether this framework is adequate is currently being debated. These current general understandings of domestic violence are worth reviewing for their relevance to gay and lesbian victims and batterers. However, study of gay and lesbian domestic violence to date, though limited, has suggested ways in which theory and practice may need to be modified.

Domestic violence is currently understood as any pattern of behavior designed to dominate, coerce, or isolate within a relationship. It is an exercise of any form of power that is used to maintain control or to dominate. This is thought to be another manifestation of sexism, an ideology of unequal power not necessarily based on gender. Since battery (according to the dominant thinking in this field) is caused by the cultural belief that hierarchical rule and coercive authority are natural, then all relationships tend to be based on power and domination. All forms of battery are linked.

> *"All over the country gay men are coming forward to seek help as victims of domestic violence."*

This lesson is strongly reinforced in the socialization of men and women; gay men, bisexuals, and lesbians are no exception. Regardless of sexual orientation, certain lessons are learned within the family. The family is a place where unequal power is evident and where that power can be used, without consequences, to control. Lesbians, like non-lesbians, often desire control over the resources and decisions in family life that power brings and that violence can assure when control is resisted. Lesbians have learned that violence works in achieving partner compliance. Therefore, B. Hart asserts that lesbian batterers abuse for much the same reason as heterosexual men do—namely, to get what they want.

Battering relationships are rarely only abusive. Love, caring, and remorse are often part of a cyclical pattern of abuse. Survivors are convinced that the situation will change for the better. They want the relationship to continue but the violence to end. As in any relationship, shame, isolation, and economic or emotional dependency can be major barriers to leaving.

The Batterers

Most scholars and practitioners fail to identify a common profile of a batterer/abuser. Most would agree that there is no provocation or justification for domestic violence. Psychotherapists when working with a lesbian batterer start with a fundamental assumption: she (the batterer) must accept responsibility for her actions and the consequences of her actions because she has chosen violence. They emphasize that the lesbian abuser is accountable not only to the survivor but to the gay community.

Theory for practice related to male domestic abuse suggests that batterers have a learned, progressive psychological disorder and will continue to act out their dysfunction until they obtain help and follow the prescribed treatment. Violence is a choice. *Social learning theory* suggests that batterers actually believe that they will "get their way" if they create an environment and atmosphere of intimidation and terror for their lover. People, according to this theory, will take repeated instances of a lesser punishment to avoid an extreme punishment that has been threatened. Positive reinforcement is involved because at the end of the violent episode, "making up" often includes sex and other expressions of affection. Once the rage has passed, the cessation of the perpetrator's violence is a reinforcement to the violent act. For the abuser, violence itself may be self-reinforcing because it serves as a tension release.

Developmental and cognitive theories are referenced by those who view the perpetrator as having experienced some developmental impairment. Specifically, the perpetrator did not learn to choose a nonviolent solution but learned to be violent toward those who do not do what he or she wants. This cognitive, developmental flaw was acquired through parental neglect, inappropriate modeling, or inept teaching by adults around them. *Personality theory* might suggest that male batterers overexaggerate their masculinity so as to validate their maleness. *Communication theory* suggests that male abusers have failed to acquire adequate communication skills, that is, the ability to verbalize anger without resorting to violence. A number of theorists view batterers as psychologically unhealthy, with a mental disorder. They contend that batterers have several characteristics that differentiate them, to some degree, from men in general. They note that batterers who were abused as children are more likely to present personality disorders and are highly resistant to treatment.

> *"Violent and abusive behavior are found in all segments of the gay and lesbian community."*

This mental health perspective on gay and lesbian domestic violence is highly controversial because it counters the prevailing view that battering is not a psychiatric issue, that if society were to change, the battering would stop. From this perspective, if domestic violence were pathologized, as has been the case with homosexuality historically, and with drug abuse and alcoholism more recently, the field would be taken over by professionals with little experience with the problem. Island and Letellier reject what they see as sexual politics, the position posed by "some women [who] fear that the use of mental disorder categories by therapists treating lesbian batterers will lead to further victimization of women, a group already damaged by incompetent, sexist, or homophobic therapists and institutions for hundreds of years." They argue that by not properly labeling the batterer as disordered, it can be interpreted that the community is aiding and abetting the perpetrator in avoiding accountability for his or her conduct.

Practice wisdom in the domestic violence field, however, assumes a contrary stance; that is, most men are viewed as violent and inherently aggressive since in 80 percent of the marriages, husbands are abusive toward their wives. This position is disputed by R.J. Gelles and M.A. Straus; they contend that some men follow a negative societal prescription for masculinity while others do not. Those who follow blindly the popular American notions of acting tough at all times, not showing tender feelings at all (e.g., the lean, mean, super cool, stoic cowboy type), those who get their way by flexing their muscles, drinking to excess, getting angry and hitting people are heading toward pain, trouble, and possible domestic violence. The behavioral idea of masculinity for some men is to intimidate, to dominate, and to do what they damn well want to, no matter what the consequences to themselves and to other people. Masculinity to these men is reflected in their attempt to control others so that they are sure that no one controls them, since being influenced by others is considered unmasculine. . . .

> *"Regardless of sexual orientation, certain lessons are learned within the family."*

America is a violent culture and a patriarchal society at its roots, yet millions of men who experience all these pervasive forces reject all of them, adopt only some of them, or dramatically neutralize most of them. *Sociopolitical theory*, which identifies causation as solely gender-role socialization and patriarchy, lets the individual violent man off the hook by not giving sufficient attention to his psychological makeup, his interpretation of "masculinity," his dysfunctional choices, and his responsibility for the criminally violent act.

The Victims

Lesbians and gay men are aware of the mistaken belief of mental health providers that the survivor's behavior reflects masochism or personal weakness or that it is caused by substance abuse, intimacy problems, family influences, stress, childhood violence, or provocation. While these may be related factors in some cases, they are not causes. Some have even questioned the division of roles in abusive relationships into a simple dichotomy of victim and perpetrator. However, most commentators find that those who are abused within an intimate relationship often manifest certain characteristics in common *at least in the context of that relationship,* such as being dependent, overly responsible, concerned with the needs and feelings of others, and feeling inferior or inadequate in the relationship. The abuse they suffer tends to reinforce and magnify these same traits. However, there is no evidence that victims of domestic abuse share any common mental health disorder or problem in every case.

Island and Letellier depart from the consensus position that there is no victim profile. They propose a victim theory which postulates that

> the prospective victim will tend to have relatively sound mental health without
> a prior history of, or contact with, abuse of any kind. This person has a history

of handling life's problems in a reasonably confident and effective manner. Many tend to blame [themselves] for most interpersonal problems with others and to absolve others. This [abused] individual may tend to want to please others and sometimes submit to control and influence by others . . . may tend to mistrust his own judgment about people and to be uneasy with disagreement, to be conciliatory, though argumentative, in response to interpersonal disagreements. This individual may tend toward taking responsibility for others; a strong sense of independence; low self-worth; a fatalistic world-view; a considerable reservoir of guilt; liking people; trust and lack of suspicion; insecurity; high ego strength; and trivializes or denies the negative or unpleasant.

These authors challenge current thinking in the domestic violence field, first by rejecting the popular notion that domestic violence is codependency, second by extending the analysis of power in relationships beyond the traditional male/female dyad, and finally by postulating that the victim and the batterer have very separate psychologies.

Views like these suggest that power, not gender, underlies lesbian and gay male abuse. Our previous discussion of cultural heterosexism helps us to understand that most gay men and lesbians were raised in heterosexual homes where power differences between men and women, parents and children fueled the gender-role socialization patterns that they may then have modeled in their own relationships. While these and other authors who write about gay and lesbian domestic violence draw heavily from all the current domestic violence literature, they differ markedly from many of the theoretical, clinical, and political positions of the pioneers in this field in that they emphasize that many propositions do not apply to lesbians and gay men. A more sophisticated understanding of domestic violence in general and in gay and lesbian relationships in particular is clearly needed in order to intervene more sensitively and effectively.

Chapter 2

Is the Prevalence of Family Violence Exaggerated?

Chapter Preface

Before 1960, only the most severe forms of abuse against children were usually reported to authorities. However, public acknowledgment that child abuse is a serious problem that should be reported has increased dramatically since then. According to researcher David Finkelhor, there has been an approximate ten percent rise in estimated number of child abuse cases per year since the 1960s. In 1990, the National Committee for the Prevention of Child Abuse (NCPCA) estimated that over 2.5 million children in the United States suffered some form of abuse or neglect. In Finkelhor's view, this increase is not evidence of a new epidemic of violence, but rather a result of increased awareness among the citizenry and public officials.

Many researchers believe, however, that the number of cases reported each year still represents only a small proportion of actual mistreated children. In fact, some studies have suggested significantly higher numbers. In 1985, for example, respected researchers Murray Strauss and Richard Gelles conducted a survey of American families and found that one in ten children were subjected to severe physical violence.

The acceptance of child abuse as a significant problem has led authorities to transform the issue from a family dilemma to a public responsibility. Researcher Douglas Besharov points out that every state now requires an array of public officials—from physicians to teachers to day care workers—to report suspected abuse. At least twenty states also require mandatory reporting by all citizens.

Yet many social scientists contend that in their efforts to raise public awareness of child abuse, some authorities exaggerate the severity of the problem. Writer Richard Wexler points to a 1988 study funded by the National Center of Child Abuse and Neglect which found that 97 percent of children are not abused or neglected in any way in the course of a year.

In his book *Wounded Innocents,* Wexler points out that many researchers cite "reported cases" of child abuse to inflate statistics and strengthen their positions. Many of these cases, writes Wexler, are instances of *alleged* abuse, not actual abuse. He recounts the nightmare experienced by James Norman, whose children were taken away after someone phoned a child abuse hotline because he could not pay his utility bill. According to Wexler, Norman's case is one of many that overzealous researchers use to pad their statistics on family violence.

The incidence of child abuse is only one area of debate regarding the prevalence of family violence. Another controversy revolves around what constitutes family violence. For example, is spanking a legitimate way to discipline a child, or is it a form of child abuse? These and other questions will be explored in the following chapter.

Violence Against Women Is Overreported

by Armin A. Brott

About the author: *Armin A. Brott is a freelance writer living in Berkeley, California, and a frequent contributor to the* Washington Post.

[Everyone remembers how the brutal murders of] Nicole Brown Simpson and Ronald Goldman . . . kept millions of Americans close to their television sets. But there's a third victim of these killings: the truth about the prevalence of domestic violence and female victimization—a truth maimed almost beyond recognition by the irresponsible use of statistics.

Domestic Violence Figures Are Questionable

Consider the wildly varying number of women who are supposedly beaten by men each year. The National Coalition Against Domestic Violence, for example, estimates that more than half of married women (over 27 million) will experience violence during their marriage, and that more than one-third (over 18 million) are battered repeatedly every year. Both statistics are widely quoted in the media.

But when I asked Rita Smith, coordinator of the NCADV, where these figures came from, she conceded that they were only "estimates." From where? "Based on what we hear out there." Out where? In battered women's shelters and from other advocacy groups.

Common sense suggests that asking women at a shelter whether they've been hit would be like asking patrons at McDonald's whether they ever eat fast food. Obviously such answers cannot be extrapolated to the country as a whole.

Government Estimates Are Also Dubious

Donna Shalala, secretary of health and human services, offers a lower but still eye-popping estimate. Four million women are battered each year by their male partners—"just about as common as giving birth," she said [in March 1994].

But where did Shalala get this figure? From a 1993 Harris poll commissioned

Reprinted from Armin Brott, "Battered Truth Syndrome," *The Washington Post*, July 31, 1994. Reprinted by permission of the author.

by the Commonwealth Fund, in which 2 percent of the 2,500 women interviewed said they had been "kicked, bit, hit with a fist or some other object." Based on about 55 million women married or living with a man, that's a total of 1.1 million. So where did the other 2.9 million come from? They were women who said they had been "pushed, grabbed, shoved or slapped"—not pleasant or condonable, certainly, but also not what most people would call the "terrorism in the home" Shalala referred to in her speech. Shalala—and media reporting the story—also neglected to tell us that fewer than 1 percent of those polled claimed ever to have been beaten up, much less choked or threatened by their partners with a knife or gun.

Shalala's statistics, however, pale in comparison to those issued by various women's advocacy groups. By far the worst distortion of the number of battered women comes from Pat Stevens, a radio talk show host who was interviewed on CNN's "Crossfire" [in June 1994]. Stevens estimated that, when adjusted for underreporting, the true number of battered women is 60 million. No one bothered to tell "Crossfire" viewers that 60 million is more than 100 percent of all the women in America who are currently in relationships with a man. Instead, Stevens's "estimate" and the other "facts" on the number of battered women serve to fuel the claims that there's an "epidemic of domestic violence" and a "war against women."

More Realistic Estimates

So how many battered women are there? Murray Straus and Richard Gelles, who have been tracking spousal abuse for more than 20 years, have come up with what are widely believed to be the most accurate estimates available—the National Family Violence Survey (NFVS).

The survey, sponsored by the National Institute of Mental Health, found that there is no violence in about 84 percent of American families. In the 16 percent of families that do experience violence, the vast majority of that violence takes the form of slapping, shoving and grabbing. This is not to minimize the violence that occurs—or the seriousness of some violence against spouses. But the fact is that only 3 to 4 percent of all families (about 1.8 million) have members who engage in "severe" violence—kicking, punching or using a weapon. And a recent study published

> *"Common sense suggests that asking women at a shelter whether they've been hit would be like asking patrons at McDonald's whether they ever eat fast food."*

in the *Archives of Internal Medicine* found that 44 percent of "severe violence" to wives did not cause any injury, and 31 percent caused only slight bruises.

Still, Straus and Gelles estimate that about 188,000 women are injured severely enough to require medical attention. That's a horrifying number, but it's a far cry from the many millions of damaged victims implied by the least cautious users of the statistics.

Another commonly accepted "truth" about domestic violence is that 95 percent of the time women are the victims—and men the perpetrators. But the NFVS—and a variety of other studies—have found that men are just as likely to be the victims of domestic violence as women. Straus and Gelles found that among couples reporting violence, the man struck the first blow in 27 percent of the cases; the woman in 24 percent. The rest of the time, the violence was mutual, with both partners brawling. The results were the same even when the most severe episodes of violence were analyzed. They were also the same when only the woman's version of the events was considered.

Even more interesting are Straus's findings . . . that men's violence against women—even as reported by women—has dropped 43 percent between 1985 and 1992. Over the same period, in contrast, assaults by women against men actually increased.

So where did the 95 percent figure come from? From the U.S. Department of Justice, which collects data on the number of reports of domestic violence. But as women's rights groups rightfully claim, reports are not always an accurate measure of the severity of the problem. Certainly, some female victims of domestic violence fail to call the police, fearing retaliation by their abusers. But other Justice Department studies have shown that men—who are socialized to "take it like a man"—report violent victimization much less frequently than women.

> *"The vast majority of [domestic] violence takes the form of slapping, shoving and grabbing."*

"They wouldn't dream of reporting the kind of minor abuse—such as slapping or kicking—that women routinely report," says Suzanne Steinmetz, director of the Family Research Institute at Indiana University/Purdue.

Other Distorted Beliefs

Yet another example of how data on female victimization are distorted is the belief that domestic violence is the most common cause of injury to women. The source for this claim is a 1991 study of extremely poor inner-city women in Philadelphia. In fact, the study did not find that domestic violence was the leading cause of injury even for this group. "And even if it did," says Jeane Ann Grisso, one of the lead researchers of the study, "I'd never apply that conclusion to the total population of American women." Nevertheless, Grisso's study has been widely cited as proof of the epidemic of violence against women.

Several studies done in the 1970s by Evan Stark and Anne Flitcraft also gave rise to another questionable claim: that as many as 50 percent of women's emergency-room admissions are the result of ongoing abuse. They compiled their data by going through medical records in urban hospitals and estimating how many women were battered by using what they called an "index of suspicion."

Christina Hoff Sommers, author of *Who Stole Feminism,* has analyzed Stark and Flitcraft's methods and writes: "If a woman was assaulted but the records do not say who hit her, Stark and Flitcraft classify this as a case of 'probable' domestic abuse; if she has injuries to her face and torso that are inadequately explained, they classify it as 'suggestive of abuse.'" That may not seem implausible but it ignores the real possibility that, in the environment studied, women may well have been victimized by drug sellers, pimps and other people they could not identify or would be afraid to identify. Or that the hospital failed to ask or record the information. Moreover, other studies do not support the finding.

> *"A variety of . . . studies . . . have found that men are just as likely to be the victims of domestic violence as women."*

Compare Stark and Flitcraft's results to those reached in a 1992 survey of 397 emergency rooms in California. Nurses were asked to estimate the number of patients per month who have been diagnosed with injuries caused by domestic violence. Estimates ranged from two per month for small hospitals to eight per month for large ones. The California study concluded that the number of perceived domestic violence victims was so low because many health professionals are poorly trained in recognizing domestic violence. They may be right, but it's doubtful that that accounts for the entire difference between a handful of domestic violence cases a month and 50 percent of all emergency room admissions.

When Domestic Violence Becomes Deadly

Distorted statistics notwithstanding, there are clearly women who have been severely battered, and many of them are afraid to leave their batterers—either because they are economically dependent or because they fear further abuse. And in another one of its highly-publicized statistics, the National Coalition Against Domestic Violence tells us that women who leave their batterers "increase by 75 percent their chances of getting killed."

When I asked Rita Smith to explain, she conceded that the coalition has no concrete evidence of the effect that leaving a violent partner will have on a woman. I asked Smith whether it bothered her that her organization was responsible for spreading an imaginary statistic. "Not really," she said. "We think the chance of getting killed goes up and we're just trying to make a point here."

In a small number of tragic cases, abusive men do kill their partners—the FBI estimates that about 1,400 women (about 6 percent of all murders) were killed by their spouses or partners in 1992, though not all of the murders were the result of escalating domestic abuse. But the impression one gets is that women are the only ones killed in domestic disputes. Again, this impression is contradicted by the facts. A Justice Department study released [in July 1994] showed that 41 percent of spousal murder victims were male. Battered-women's advocates claim that those women who kill their husbands do so only out of self-defense. But in an extensive study of women imprisoned for murder, researcher Coramae Richey Mann found that over 40 percent did not claim they acted in self-defense and 30 percent had previously been arrested for violent crimes. Nor is it the case that female spouse murderers are treated more harshly than their male counterparts. . . . Justice Department statistics show that women convicted of killing their partners receive an average sentence of only six years; men get 17.

Distorted Statistics Are Not Harmless

Why are these statistics being abused? Obviously some of the data abusers do so with the best of intentions. They are simply trying to get people to sit up and pay attention to the plight of battered women—a truly important goal. But to do so, they've created a false epidemic. If advocates had confined themselves to the truth, domestic violence might have continued to be regarded as a serious, yet curable, problem. But if 19 or 50 or even 100 percent of women are "brutalized," a much more sweeping conclusion is suggested: that all men are dangerous and that all women need to be protected.

This raises age-old ethical dilemmas. Is it okay to lie if your cause is a noble one? After all, distortions about the extent of domestic violence have had some positive effects, opening the public's eyes as well as their wallets. Battered women are now the hottest story in town; . . . Congress [passed] the $1.8 billion Violence Against Women Act [in 1994] which, among other things, will fund toll-free hotlines, battered women's shelters and education and training programs. It's certainly possible that none of this would be happening if advocacy groups stuck strictly to the facts.

Consequences of Abused Statistics

Yet even supposedly harmless "puffing" can have negative consequences. Having fought so hard to be taken seriously and treated as equals, women are again finding themselves portrayed as weak and helpless—the stereotypes that have been traditionally used to justify discriminating against them. As author Katherine Dunn writes, "The denial of female aggression is a destructive myth. It robs an entire gender of a significant spectrum of power, leaving women less than equal with men and effectively keeping them 'in their place' and under control."

But perhaps the worst consequence of the inflation of domestic violence statistics is that a type of ratchet effect develops: The same people who complain that no one listens if they don't exaggerate only find it more difficult to get people's attention the next time around, thus "justifying" yet another inflation. Eventually, the public either stops listening altogether or finds the statistics too absurd to believe. And when we're trying to alleviate the tragedy of domestic violence, the last thing you want anyone to do is laugh.

Child Abuse Is Overreported

by Shaun Asseal

About the author: *Shaun Asseal is a father as well as an investigative reporter who covers law and crime.*

[The year is 1995.] Stephanie Timm, a 3-year-old with curly brown hair that ripples luxuriantly down her back, opens her mouth to talk, but the words don't come. Instead, she makes a sound like a billy goat, ebullient but shrill.

Just two years [prior], Stephanie was starting to speak when she and her two brothers were summarily removed from their family home. The reason: an accusation of child abuse brought against the children's mother, Teresa Timm, by a former friend with an ax to grind.

A Cloudy Issue

The clash that followed between the Timm family and the child-welfare officials of Cass County, Nebraska, has brought attention to a family-justice system where definitions of abuse and neglect are so murky that no one seems to agree on what they mean.

As a result, politicians, legal experts, and psychologists are asking how they can better protect the rights of parents while saving children from real harm.

Teresa and Jeff Timm are fourth-generation family farmers in Murdock, Nebraska. Teresa was pregnant with their fourth child when, on June 16, 1993, two patrol cars followed her along a dirt road as she was driving home from an OB-GYN visit. The officers were on their way to remove her three kids—Tony, then 5; Justin, 2½; and Stephanie, 11 months. A woman who had been turned down by the Timms for a $7,000 loan had filed a written report accusing Teresa of child abuse. The report twisted facts, such as Teresa's frequently taking her kids to emergency rooms, into claims that she was violent.

The Children Are Taken

The Nebraska Department of Social Services assigned a 27-year-old social worker with just one year's experience to investigate. She was joined by two sheriff's deputies, one of whom had been to the Timm home a year earlier in-

Reprinted from Shaun Asseal, "Child Abuse: Guilty Until Proven Innocent," *Parents*, July 1995. Reprinted by permission of the author.

vestigating Teresa's report of a burglary in progress. Because no evidence of the break-in was ever found, Michael Rumbaugh, general counsel of the Nebraska Department of Social Services, said the social worker and the deputies thought they were "dealing with someone whose credibility in the community was suspect." Teresa, who insists her report was truthful, says the social worker "had her mind made up" when she arrived at the Timms' home and drove off with the children.

The first separation was brief. By the next dawn, the family's lawyer had contacted the county attorney and had them returned. But the following week a hearing was held before a county court judge, which under Nebraska law the Timms were not required to be told about. According to a transcript, the social worker said that Tony talked about being "fearful of his mother when she was angry and yelling at him." The court had copies of the family medical records, which, Rumbaugh says, suggested that Teresa "could be a classic overuser of medical resources." Tony's chronic asthma was not mentioned.

A Second Separation

Although the county attorney recommended removing the Timm children, he revealed uneasiness. "This is not what I consider to be real firm," he remarked.

On June 23, 1993, two sheriff's cars again raced up the dirt road. Teresa remembers the scene this way:

"Jeff's face went white. I said, 'God help me, how can you do this to my kids?' Tony started crying and clawing my shirt. Justin was saying, 'No, Mommy, don't make me go. I'll be good.' I was thinking, 'Why don't they make me move away? Why are they taking the kids from Jeff?'"

Over the next three and a half weeks, as the children were placed first in foster care, then with their grandparents, the county's case began to unravel. After a psychiatric evaluation of Teresa, the case was dismissed. The children came home.

Now Teresa Timm is suing the county and state for $10 million. She says her children are haunted by nightmares, Tony suffers from depression, and Stephanie is speech-delayed. "In Nebraska," she says, "if someone screams child abuse, you're guilty until proven innocent."

Judith Sheindlin [television's Judge Judy], supervising judge of the family court in New York County, is asked how the legal system can prevent the unnecessary separation of children from families when a report is wrongly substantiated. She responds with a story from her days

> *"Politicians, legal experts, and psychologists are asking how they can better protect the rights of parents while saving children from real harm."*

as a judge in the Bronx in the mid-1980s. At that time there was a spate of sex-abuse cases in which young girls were diagnosed with chlamydia, a sexually transmitted disease.

"I had a problem believing that some of the men I saw would sexually abuse their children," Sheindlin remembers. "And if you make a judgment that is wrong, you are permanently removing this man from his child's life. Down the line no one will feel comfortable letting him go back into his child's house."

Sheindlin conducted her own investigation and discovered that there were two types of tests done for chlamydia—a cheap, error-prone 24-hour test and a more expensive five-day test. A private lab was doing the cheaper test and billing the city for the more expensive one. Sheindlin blew the whistle and dismissed dozens of tainted cases. In the decade since, she says, only a handful of new ones have been filed. What resonates about the story today is that, as Sheindlin puts it, "there are still insufficient protocols that are uniformly applied."

Soft Evidence Leaves Room for Error

Of roughly 3 million abuse and neglect reports logged every year, about 66 percent are not substantiated after investigation, according to a 1993 survey by the National Committee for the Prevention of Child Abuse. That leaves about 1 million cases that are substantiated, most with a finding of "some credible evidence."

What is meant by "some credible evidence"? In about 40 percent of those million cases, sexual and physical abuse can be shown by such means as X rays, radiology reports, or rape tests.

Most of the remaining 60 percent—about 600,000 cases a year—

"Of roughly 3 million abuse and neglect reports logged every year, about 66 percent are not substantiated after investigation."

involve a caseworker entering a parent's home and making a subjective decision that a child is not getting adequate care, food, or shelter. If even a fraction of those judgments result from misunderstandings, tens of thousands of families are being wrongly separated.

Circumstantial Cases Are Becoming Too Common

"It's a terrible problem," says Edward Zigler, Ph.D., the Sterling Professor of Psychology at Yale University. He cites a case in New Haven in which social workers removed a child from his home after noticing blotches on the child's leg, even though the parents had a doctor's report attesting to the presence of a blood disorder. The Department of Social Services was convinced the blotches were a by-product of abuse. "It took much too long to get the child back," he says.

Zigler worries that circumstantial cases built on soft evidence are becoming all too common. "I see an expansion of parental behaviors that are classified as abuse. Now people are talking about emotional abuse—if you yell at your child, is that abuse? I think we're wasting our time labeling everyone. The whole area has become too subjective."

Richard Wexler, the author of *Wounded Innocents* (Prometheus Books), which looks at civil-liberties abuses in the family-court system, argues that much of what is currently called neglect is actually poverty. "I'm talking about a family where the food stamps run out," says Wexler. "Or it could be a lack-of-supervision case where the mother is trying to hold down two jobs and the baby-sitter doesn't come through. My research shows that twice as many children are being removed from their homes as should be."

> *"We need to be better skilled in determining which reports of child abuse and neglect are valid, and then intervene appropriately."*

The solution, according to Howard Davidson, director of the American Bar Association's Center on Children and the Law, is "a more professionalized child-protection intervention system. We need to be better skilled in determining which reports of child abuse and neglect are valid, and then intervene appropriately."

The Child's Testimony May Be Unreliable

When children do enter the family-justice system, they often become disoriented. "After a child tells the story a half dozen times to people who may or may not be trained, all the subtle innuendo is lost," says New York's Judge Sheindlin.

One of the most infamous cases of a child's testimony changing 180 degrees during an investigation involved the daughter of a 40-year-old San Diego man named James Wade. Wade was charged with sexually abusing the girl, even though she initially told police that she was abducted from her home by a stranger and raped. By the time therapists finished their interviews, she was saying her father had done it. Further DNA testing ruled out Wade's involvement, and charges against him were dropped.

The Wade case helped produce what may have been the first election in which prosecutorial overzealousness in child-abuse cases was a factor. [In November 1994,] San Diego voters replaced their district attorney of 24 years with newcomer Paul Pfingst, who, in one of his first acts in office, ordered a review of dozens of pending child-abuse cases to make sure that "we're not using soft science to overcome gaps in evidence."

Reforming the System

Cases like those of Wade and Timm have sparked a reform movement aimed at correcting some of the excesses of the past decade.

- In Chicago, $1.8 million of state funds are allocated among social-service agencies to help parents who are separated from their children because of inadequate housing. The Norman Fund is named after a man who tried to keep his children together after his wife died. But they were placed in foster care because a caseworker determined that his house was too "messy." He died 12 days before the case was finally going to be heard.

- The city of Louisville, Kentucky, has developed a national model for investigating abuse reports using trained teams of police and social workers. "Courts are only as good as the accuracy of the information they're presented," says Judge Richard Fitzgerald, who helped develop the new system. The model will be in use throughout Kentucky by decade's end.
- Advocates are beginning to call for amendments to state laws that protect anyone who anonymously makes a child-abuse report. "All they'd have to do is say that malicious reports are subject to civil lawsuits, and a lot of it would stop," says Joe Dolphin, president of the Board of Governors of the California Community Colleges, who headed a San Diego grand-jury review of abuse cases. A bill that would make malicious reporting a crime failed to be voted on in Congress last year.

For D.A. Paul Pfingst, the mandate is clear. He says, "We're removing children from their parents too often, and too aggressively, without sustainable evidence. That's got to stop. We've got to take a good hard look at where we are and make some changes."

Child Abuse Is Underreported or Misreported

by Douglas J. Besharov and Lisa A. Laumann

About the authors: *Douglas J. Besharov is a resident scholar at the American Enterprise Institute for Public Policy Research and former director of the U.S. National Center on Child Abuse and Neglect. Lisa A. Laumann assisted Dr. Besharov with the preparation of this viewpoint while serving as a research assistant at the American Enterprise Institute.*

For 30 years, advocates, program administrators, and politicians have joined to encourage even more reports of suspected child abuse and neglect. Their efforts have been spectacularly successful, with about three million cases of suspected child abuse having been reported in 1993. Large numbers of endangered children still go unreported, but an equally serious problem has developed: Upon investigation, as many as 65 percent of the reports now being made are determined to be "unsubstantiated," raising serious civil liberties concerns and placing a heavy burden on already overwhelmed investigative staffs.

These two problems—nonreporting and inappropriate reporting—are linked and must be addressed together before further progress can be made in combating child abuse and neglect. To lessen both problems, there must be a shift in priorities—away from simply seeking more reports and toward encouraging better reports.

Reporting Laws

Since the early 1960s, all states have passed laws that require designated professionals to report specified types of child maltreatment. Over the years, both the range of designated professionals and the scope of reportable conditions have been steadily expanded.

Initially, mandatory reporting laws applied only to physicians, who were required to report only "serious physical injuries" and "nonaccidental injuries." In the ensuing years, however, increased public and professional attention, sparked in part by the number of abused children revealed by these initial reporting laws, led many states to expand their reporting requirements. Now almost all states have laws that require the reporting of all forms of suspected child maltreatment, including physical abuse, physical neglect, emotional maltreatment, and, of course, sexual abuse and exploitation.

Under threat of civil and criminal penalties, these laws require most professionals who serve children to report suspected child abuse and neglect. About twenty states require all citizens to report, but in every state, any citizen is permitted to report.

Reports Increase

These reporting laws, associated public awareness campaigns, and professional education programs have been strikingly successful. In 1993, there were about three million reports of children suspected of being abused or neglected. This is a twenty-fold increase since 1963, when about 150,000 cases were reported to the authorities. (As we will see, however, this figure is bloated by reports that later turn out to be unfounded.)

> *"There must be a shift in priorities—away from simply seeking more [child abuse] reports and toward encouraging better reports."*

Many people ask whether this vast increase in reporting signals a rise in the incidence of child maltreatment. Recent increases in social problems such as out-of-wedlock births, inner-city poverty, and drug abuse have probably raised the underlying rates of child maltreatment, at least somewhat. Unfortunately, so many maltreated children previously went unreported that earlier reporting statistics do not provide a reliable baseline against which to make comparisons. One thing is clear, however: The great bulk of reports now received by child protective agencies would not be made but for the passage of mandatory reporting laws and the media campaigns that accompanied them.

Child Protective Programs

This increase in reporting was accompanied by a substantial expansion of prevention and treatment programs. Every community, for example, is now served by specialized child protective agencies that receive and investigate reports. Federal and state expenditures for child protective programs and associated foster care services now exceed $6 billion a year. . . .

As a result, many thousands of children have been saved from serious injury and even death. The best estimate is that over the past twenty years, child abuse and neglect deaths have fallen from over 3,000 a year—and perhaps as many as 5,000—to about 1,100 a year. In New York State, for example, within five years of the passage of a comprehensive reporting law, which also created specialized investigative staffs, there was a 50 percent reduction in child fatalities, from about two hundred a year to less than one hundred. . . .

Unreported Cases

Most experts agree that reports have increased over the past thirty years because professionals and laypersons have become more likely to report apparently abusive and neglectful situations. But the question remains: How many more cases still go unreported?

Two studies performed for the National Center on Child Abuse and Neglect by Westat, Inc., provide a partial answer. In 1980 and then again in 1986, Westat conducted national studies of the incidence of child abuse and neglect. . . . Each study used essentially the same methodology: In a stratified sample of counties, a broadly representative sample of professionals who serve children was asked whether, during the study period, the children they had seen in their professional capacities appeared to have been abused or neglected. . . .

"The great bulk of reports now being received . . . would not be made but for the passage of mandatory reporting laws and the media campaigns that accompany them."

Westat found that professionals failed to report many of the children they saw who had observable signs of child abuse and neglect. Specifically, it found that in 1986, 56 percent of apparently abused or neglected children, or about 500,000 children, were not reported to the authorities. This figure, however, seems more alarming than it is: Basically, the more serious the case, the more likely the report. For example, the surveyed professionals reported over 85 percent of the fatal or serious physical abuse cases they saw, 72 percent of the sexual abuse cases, and 60 percent of the moderate physical abuse cases. In contrast, they only reported 15 percent of the educational neglect cases they saw, 24 percent of the emotional neglect cases, and 25 percent of the moderate physical neglect cases.

Nevertheless, there is no reason for complacency. Translating these raw percentages into actual cases means that in 1986, about 2,000 children with observable physical injuries severe enough to require hospitalization were not reported and that more than 100,000 children with moderate physical injuries went unreported, as did more than 30,000 apparently sexually abused children. And these are the rates of nonreporting among relatively well-trained professionals. One assumes that nonreporting is higher among less-well-trained professionals and higher still among laypersons.

Inappropriate Reports Confuse the Issue

Obtaining and maintaining a high level of reporting requires a continuation of the public education and professional training begun thirty years ago. But, now, such efforts must also address a problem as serious as nonreporting: inappropriate reporting.

At the same time that many seriously abused children go unreported, an equally serious problem further undercuts efforts to prevent child maltreatment: The nation's child protective agencies are being inundated by inappropriate reports. Although rules, procedures, and even terminology

> *"The nation's child protective agencies are being inundated by inappropriate reports."*

vary—some states use the phrase "unfounded," others "unsubstantiated" or "not indicated"—an "unfounded" report, in essence, is one that is dismissed after an investigation finds insufficient evidence upon which to proceed.

Nationwide, between 60 and 65 percent of all reports are closed after an initial investigation determines that they are "unfounded" or "unsubstantiated." This is in sharp contrast to 1974, when only about 45 percent of all reports were unfounded.

A few advocates, in a misguided effort to shield child protective programs from criticism, have sought to quarrel with estimates that I and others have made that the national unfounded rate is between 60 and 65 percent. They have grasped at various inconsistencies in the data collected by different organizations to claim either that the problem is not so bad or that it has always been this bad.

To help settle this dispute, the American Public Welfare Association (APWA) conducted a special survey of child welfare agencies in 1989. The APWA researchers found that between fiscal year 1986 and fiscal year 1988, the weighted average for the substantiation rates in thirty-one states declined 6.7 percent—from 41.8 percent in fiscal year 1986 to 39 percent in fiscal year 1988.

Most recently, the existence of this high unfounded rate was reconfirmed by the annual Fifty State Survey of the National Committee to Prevent Child Abuse (NCPCA), which found that in 1993 only about 34 percent of the reports received by child protective agencies were substantiated.

The experience of New York City indicates what these statistics mean in practice. Between 1989 and 1993, as the number of reports received by the city's child welfare agency increased by over 30 percent (from 40,217 to 52,472), the percentage of substantiated reports fell by about 47 percent (from 45 percent to 24 percent). In fact, the number of substantiated cases—a number of families were reported more than once—actually fell by about 41 percent, from 14,026 to 8,326. Thus, 12,255 additional families were investigated, while 5,700 fewer families received child protective help.

A Breach of Privacy

The determination that a report is unfounded can only be made after an unavoidably traumatic investigation that is inherently a breach of parental and

family privacy. To determine whether a particular child is in danger, caseworkers must inquire into the most intimate personal and family matters. Often it is
necessary to question friends, relatives, and neighbors, as well as school teachers, day-care personnel, doctors, clergy, and others who know the family.

Laws against child abuse are an implicit recognition that family privacy must
give way to the need to protect helpless children. But in seeking to protect children, it is all too easy to ignore the legitimate rights of parents. Each year,
about 700,000 families are put through investigations of unfounded reports.
This is a massive and unjustified violation of parental rights.

Most Reports Are Well-Intentioned

Few unfounded reports are made maliciously. Studies of sexual abuse reports,
for example, suggest that, at most, from 4 to 10 percent of these reports are
knowingly false. Many involve situations in which the person reporting, in a
well-intentioned effort to protect a child, overreacts to a vague and often mis-
leading possibility that the child may be maltreated. Others involve situations
of poor child care that, though of legitimate concern, simply do not amount to
child abuse or neglect. In fact, a substantial proportion of unfounded cases are
referred to other agencies for them to provide needed services for the family.

Moreover, an unfounded report does not necessarily mean that the child was
not actually abused or neglected. Evidence of child maltreatment is hard to obtain and might not be uncovered when agencies lack the time and resources to
complete a thorough investigation or when inaccurate information is given to
the investigator. Other cases are labeled unfounded when no services are available to help the family. Some cases must be closed because the child or family
cannot be located.

Flood of Unfounded Reports Is Overwhelming

A certain proportion of unfounded reports, therefore, is an inherent—and legitimate—aspect of reporting *suspected* child maltreatment and is necessary to
ensure adequate child protection. Hundreds of thousands of strangers report their suspicions; they cannot all be right. But unfounded rates of the current magnitude go beyond anything reasonably needed. Worse, they endanger children who are really abused.

> *"Laws against child abuse are an implicit recognition that family privacy must give way to the need to protect helpless children."*

The current flood of unfounded reports is overwhelming the limited resources
of child protective agencies. For fear of missing even one abused child, workers
perform extensive investigations of vague and apparently unsupported reports.
Even when a home visit based on an anonymous report turns up no evidence of
maltreatment, they usually interview neighbors, school teachers, and day-care

personnel to make sure that the child is not abused. And even repeated anonymous and unfounded reports do not prevent a further investigation. But all this takes time.

Abused Children Are Lost in the Shuffle

As a result, children in real danger are getting lost in the press of inappropriate cases. Forced to allocate a substantial portion of their limited resources to unfounded reports, child protective agencies are less able to respond promptly and effectively when children are in serious danger. Some reports are left uninvestigated for a week and even two weeks after they are received. Investigations often miss key facts, as workers rush to clear cases, and dangerous home situations receive inadequate supervision, as workers must ignore pending cases as they investigate the new reports that arrive daily on their desks. Decision making also suffers. With so many cases of unsubstantiated or unproven risk to children, caseworkers are desensitized to the obvious warning signals of immediate and serious danger.

> *"An unfounded report does not necessarily mean that the child was not actually abused or neglected."*

These nationwide conditions help explain why from 25 to 50 percent of child abuse deaths involve children previously known to the authorities. In 1993, the NCPCA reported that of the 1,149 child maltreatment deaths, 42 percent had already been reported to the authorities. Tens of thousands of other children suffer serious injuries short of death while under child protective agency supervision.

Jeffrey's Case

In a 1992 New York City case, for example, five-month-old Jeffrey Harden died from burns caused by scalding water and three broken ribs while under the supervision of New York City's Child Welfare Administration. Jeffrey Harden's family had been known to the administration for more than a year and a half. Over this period, the case had been handled by four separate caseworkers, each conducting only partial investigations before resigning or being reassigned to new cases. It is unclear whether Jeffrey's death was caused by his mother or her boyfriend, but because of insufficient time and overburdened caseloads, all four workers failed to pay attention to a whole host of obvious warning signals: Jeffrey's mother had broken her parole for an earlier conviction of child sexual abuse, she had a past record of beating Jeffrey's older sister, and she had a history of crack addiction and past involvement with violent boyfriends.

Here is how two of the Hardens' caseworkers explained what happened: Their first caseworker could not find Ms. Harden at the address she had listed in her files. She commented, "It was an easy case. We couldn't find the mother so we closed it." Their second caseworker stated that he was unable to spend a sufficient amount of time investigating the case, let alone make the minimum monthly visits because he was tied down with an overabundance of cases and paperwork. He stated, "It's impossible to visit these people within a month. They're all over New York City." Just before Jeffrey's death every worker who had been on the case had left the department. Ironically, by weakening the system's ability to respond, unfounded reports actually discourage appropriate ones. The sad fact is that many responsible individuals are not reporting endangered children because they feel that the system's response will be so weak that reporting will do no good or may even make things worse. In 1984, a study of the impediments to reporting conducted by Jose Alfaro, coordinator of the New York City Mayor's Task Force on Child Abuse and Neglect, concluded that "professionals who emphasize their professional judgment, have experienced problems in dealing with the child protective agency, and are more likely to doubt the efficacy of protective service intervention, are more likely not to report in some situations, especially when they believe they can do a better job helping the family."

A Reactionary Mood

The emotionally charged desire to "do something" about child abuse, fanned by repeated and often sensational media coverage, has led to an understandable but counterproductive overreaction on the part of the professionals and citizens who report suspected child abuse. For thirty years, advocates, program administrators, and politicians have all pushed for more reporting of suspected child abuse and neglect.

Potential reporters are frequently told to "take no chances" and to report any child for whom they have the slightest concern. There is a recent tendency to tell people to report

> *"Children in real danger are getting lost in the press of inappropriate cases."*

children whose behavior suggests that they may have been abused—even in the absence of any other evidence of maltreatment. These "behavioral indicators" include, for example, children who are unusually withdrawn or shy as well as children who are unusually friendly to strangers. However, only a small minority of children who exhibit such behaviors have actually been maltreated.

Thirty years ago, even fifteen years ago, when many professionals were construing their reporting obligations narrowly to avoid taking action to protect endangered children, this approach may have been needed. Now, though, all it does is ensure that child abuse hotlines will be flooded with inappropriate and unfounded reports.

Sibling Abuse Is Underreported

by Vernon R. Wiehe

About the author: *Vernon R. Wiehe is professor in the College of Social Work at the University of Kentucky and the author of* Sibling Abuse: Hidden Physical, Emotional, and Sexual Trauma, *from which this viewpoint is excerpted.*

I was raped when I was 13 years of age—not by a stranger in a dark alley but by my own brother in my own home when he was baby-sitting me and my younger siblings. He threatened to kill me and make it look like an accident if I ever told my parents. I didn't tell, and he used me sexually from then on whenever he wanted.

I would tell my parents about how my brother would hit me. "You must have done something to deserve it," they would say. I didn't do anything. He constantly was beating me. If I tried to protect myself or hit him in return, it was proof to them I deserved it. I spent a lot of time hiding from him to protect myself.

Recently, I was with a group of friends and we were telling about nicknames we had as children. I said I didn't have any nicknames, but all the while we were laughing and talking, the name I was called by my sister kept going around in my head—*lard ass*. I wouldn't tell them that is how I was known in my house to my sister when I was a child. My parents used to laugh about it. I wasn't laughing; I was crying. My childhood was a nightmare. I don't even want to look at pictures of when I was a child. I threw my school pictures away. The memories hurt so much. At the age of 42 I have finally found the courage to seek counseling. Maybe I can come out of my shell and enjoy the remaining years of my life.

These are neither quotations from the script of a play nor words of characters of a novel. They are the comments of adults who as children were victims of a type of abuse that has largely remained undetected—sibling abuse. While considerable progress has been made in the field of family violence in detecting, treating, and preventing different types of abuse—child, spouse, or elder—one type of abuse remains largely undetected. This is the physical, emotional, and sexual abuse of one sibling by another.

Sibling Abuse Has Been Ignored

During past years, parents have excused sibling abuse in various ways. Some have looked the other way. Other parents have ignored the problem, or they wouldn't believe their children when they were told what was happening. Some have blamed the victims for the abuse they experienced—as if they were asking for it or deserved what they experienced. Still others have said it was normal behavior, simply sibling rivalry, and that this was a normal part of growing up.

Ask the survivors if they would agree that sibling abuse is typical behavior of children when they are growing up, that it is merely sibling rivalry, or that they deserved what happened to them. A resounding *No* would be heard from around the country. . . .

Ignoring sibling abuse, pretending it doesn't exist, believing the problem will solve itself, or blaming the victim for the abuse are inappropriate ways of coping with this problem. . . . The adult lives of . . . survivors are scarred both from their abuse from a sibling and from their parents' response to the abuse: They are fearful of others; feel they can trust no one; have very low self-esteem; are having problems with drugs and alcohol; and exhibit serious sexual problems.

Historical Perspective

During the past several decades, various types of family violence—child abuse, spouse abuse, elder abuse—have been brought out into the open from behind the closed doors of the family home. As these types of abuse have become known and understood, organizations and resources have developed to combat them.

While progress has been made in detecting, preventing, and treating these types of family violence, sibling abuse has largely remained unrecognized. Several reasons may be cited for this. First, there has been a reluctance for the government through its legislative bodies, the courts, police, and social service agencies to concern itself with what happens in the privacy of the home. Americans value highly their freedom. This includes the freedom to raise their children according to their religious and social values. Thus, historically the philosophy has developed, "What happens at home is the family's business." The published findings of [a 1980] study [by researchers M. Straus, R. Gelles, and S. Steinmetz on] violence in American families, based on a sample of over 2,000 families, was aptly titled, *Behind Closed Doors*.

> *"One type of abuse remains largely undetected. This is the physical, emotional, and sexual abuse of one sibling by another."*

However, the philosophy that the home is a man's castle and what happens

63

behind the closed front door is no one else's business has been challenged, and rightly so, by individuals who have been victims of abuse in their own homes — children abused by their parents, women battered by their husbands, senior citizens mistreated by their adult children. Adult survivors of child abuse, for example, have worked through the media to bring to public attention the malnutrition, beatings, sexual molestation, and death of innocent children. Legislation was passed by Congress in 1974 in the form of the Child Abuse Prevention and Treatment Act (Public Law 93-247) that among other things provided funds to the states for combating and preventing child abuse. This legislation made the reporting of incidents of child abuse mandatory and provided protection to the individual doing the reporting. Spouse abuse likewise has come to public attention in part through the efforts of the feminist movement and through the criminalization of domestic violence cases, beginning in the 1970s. States have formed adult protective service agencies for the reporting and adjudication of incidents of elder abuse. Consequently, the *closed door* of the family home is now open to the scrutiny of the court and allied agencies when the abuse of any family member is suspected. A better understanding has arisen regarding limitations to the authority of parents and other caregivers.

> *"The adult lives of . . . survivors are scarred both from their abuse from a sibling and from their parents' response to the abuse."*

Sibling Abuse Remains Unrecognized

Unfortunately, this has not been true for sibling abuse. This problem has not yet been brought out into the open. Its symptoms go unrecognized, and its devastating effects continue to be ignored. Generally, violent acts between siblings do not come to the attention of the courts unless a parent or the victim is willing to file assault charges against the perpetrating sibling. The latter rarely occurs.

There is a second reason why sibling abuse has been ignored. The abusive behavior of one sibling toward another is often excused by parents as normal behavior: "Kids will be kids"; "All kids call each other names"; "Didn't you ever play doctor when you were a child?"; "It's just normal sibling rivalry." Professionals in the field of mental health, too, have been guilty of viewing abusive behavior between siblings as part of the normal process of growing up. The behaviors to which these statements refer do occur in many families. However, these statements are inappropriate when they are used to excuse the physical, emotional, or sexual *abuse* of one sibling by another. A differentiation must be made between *sibling rivalry* and *sibling abuse*.

Approximately four decades ago child abuse was recognized. This doesn't mean that there was no child abuse before that time. It was occurring, but it was not recognized as abuse. In 1962, an article titled "The Battered Child Syndrome" was published by Dr. C. Henry Kempe and his colleagues at the University of Colorado Medical Center. This article, which would prove to have a historical impact in the field of family violence, was written by physicians who had seen many victims of child abuse. They coined the phrase *battered-child syndrome* as a clinical condition to describe the fractures, burns, wounds, and bruises they saw in their young patients as a result of physical abuse.

[In 1986] John Demos, a historian of the family, commented on the historical impact of this article:

> Child abuse evoked an immediate and complex mix of emotions: horror, shame, fascination, disgust. Dr. Kempe and his coauthors noted that physicians themselves experienced "great difficulty . . . in believing that parents could have attacked their children" and often attempted "to obliterate such suspicions from their minds, even in the face of obvious circumstantial evidence." In a sense the problem had long been consigned to a netherworld of things felt but not seen, known but not acknowledged. The "Battered Child" essay was like a shroud torn suddenly aside. Onlookers reacted with shock, but also perhaps with a kind of relief. The horror was in the open now, and it would not easily be shut up again [John Demos].

The time has come for the shroud to be torn aside on yet another type of abuse—the physical, emotional, or sexual abuse of one sibling by another. Professionals may have seen this abuse in families with whom they have worked; they may have seen the effects in adults who have sought help for their problems-in-living, but they were not able to link the effects to the cause. Perhaps they remain unsure of how to recognize this form of abuse or how to prevent it.

Chapter 3

What Are the Causes of Family Violence?

Chapter Preface

Many researchers attribute the causes of family violence to pathological or personality disorders in the abusers. From this viewpoint, violent behavior is a reaction to some buried emotional scar from the abuser's past: a son is beaten by his father, he represses the emotions, he grows up and enters a relationship, and he plays out the same scenario on his wife and children.

Others believe that violent behavior in the family is caused largely by stressful events. Perhaps a man loses his job or his wife cooks him the wrong dinner, and he reacts with violence. Many times the abusive behavior will be a completely irrational response to the triggering event.

In actuality, both perspectives are probably valid regarding the causes of violence in the family. In his book *Battered Wives*, writer Del Martin recounts a story uncovered by researcher Tracy Johnson:

> Adam and his wife Julia met in college and married after a short courtship. From the beginning they had a strange relationship. Adam saw himself as the genius in charge of the "long-range plans." Being the woman, Julia was to do the "immediate work" of earning the living, keeping house, and paying the bills. However, she failed to uphold her end of the bargain. Although she did support them during most of their marriage, she did not keep the house clean and she never managed to balance the budget. So Adam hit her. "I wanted her to take seriously the things I expected to be taken seriously," he explained. Adam also hit Julia when she said "something stupid." When he tried to control Julia's smoking and she defied him, he hit her because he was "trying to help her discipline herself."

Although Adam was a highly intelligent man who was raised in a happy home, Johnson discovered that he had developed an arrogant personality at an early age to compensate for his small and delicate stature. Much of his abusive behavior might be attributed to his need to mask his underlying sense of inadequacy. However, the behavior was undeniably triggered by events that occurred between the couple. In this abusive relationship, both the underlying psychology of the abuser and victim and the relationship sparks that occurred between them contributed to the abuse.

Researchers studying the causes of family violence also consider other factors, such as substance abuse, financial stress, and mental illness. The following chapter offers viewpoints by several leading researchers on this issue.

Unequal Gender Roles Contribute to Family Violence

by Ginny NiCarthy

About the author: *Ginny NiCarthy is a therapist, an activist in the movement to end violence against women, and the author of several self-help books for victims of abuse.*

The Masculine Role

What does it mean to be a man? Therapists questioned in a 1968 survey said that the healthy mature man is very aggressive, dominant, self-confident, independent, active, competitive, decisive, knows the ways of the world, is not easily influenced nor excitable in minor crises, and when he is emotional he almost always hides it. Some therapists have changed their attitudes since the survey was made, but many have not.

Imagine for a moment what it's like for a man to try to live up to that image. The definition of masculinity is fostered directly and indirectly by all of our institutions: the church and the government assume the man to be the authoritative and financial head of the household; schools picture males as adventurous, strong and brave in primary readers and high school history textbooks; television shows depict men as violent and powerful.

Families Reinforce the Male Role

Family members support the notion that even newborn male infants are better coordinated, more alert, hardier and stronger than female infants. It's ironic that even though most people believe males are born with certain traits, all institutions put pressure on males to develop those same traits and punish those who don't conform. No one explains why the social pressure is necessary if that's the way males naturally are. It's considered appropriate and necessary for even very young boys to be active, brave, competitive and strong, and to hide their emotions. Parents are proud when their male toddler holds back his tears and picks himself up from a fall, and they're pleased when their son persists in sticking out a game without tears or complaint, even though he's hurt by a ball or another player. He's rewarded for his bravery and physical toughness and punished if he acts "like a sissy" or "like a girl" or a coward.

Boys may be given a general message not to fight, but they're also taught, as a matter of pride, never to let another boy get away with hitting them. "Don't fight, but if you're hit first, fight back."

Boys dream of being famous race car drivers, boxers or football heroes but as they grow older it becomes more and more difficult to live up to the image of the dominant, worldly, self-confident, aggressive, decisive male. How does a person pull that off if he's sixteen years old—or twenty-three or forty-five—and he's rarely left the town where he grew up, he's never had a permanent job, or if he knows he's stuck in the tedious job he's held for twenty years? What does he do when he feels weak, vulnerable or dependent? Or when he doesn't know how to do what needs to be done—whether it's fixing the stopped-up kitchen sink, finding his way in a strange city or handling a financial problem?

The Suppression of Feelings

Many men, faced with a threat to their masculine image, try to hide their fears in bluff and bluster. They act as if they're confident and strong, independent and competent, regardless of how they feel. Sometimes this bravado helps them learn to perform tasks well. But, when they can't perform up to their standards of masculinity, they may lash out verbally or physically, blaming whoever is handy, in order to save face. In either case the unacceptable feelings of helplessness, weakness, dependency or incompetency are buried in a seemingly safe place, beneath conscious awareness. A great deal of pain is buried with them.

These feelings of failure or inadequacy are experienced by many men who have both low and high status

> *"Family members support the notion that even newborn male infants are better coordinated, more alert, hardier and stronger than female infants."*

jobs and include some who give the impression of self-confidence. Often it is only his wife who knows how vulnerable such a man feels and how fearful he is of being found out to be less than the ideal of masculinity.

A few men are fortunate enough to have been allowed and even encouraged as youngsters to express the "nonmasculine" traits of dependency, vulnerability, and emotionality. Others learn to do that as adults, through hard work and the courage to risk feeling vulnerable. In either case they'll be able to face problems with a realistic assessment of the challenge and to accept their fears and hopes about their capacity to meet it.

Why Men Batter

Why would a man use the person he loves as a punching bag? It's a cliche that there's a fine line between love and hate and that "You always hurt the one you love." Intimate relationships cause some people to feel vulnerable and dependent. If one person loves or seems to love more than the other, those feelings will be exaggerated in the one who loves most and will contribute to his or her giving the partner power. Many of us feel hostility toward those who have power over us. For men, who aren't supposed to be either dependent or powerless, love sometimes produces feelings of resentment, even rage, especially when the loved one who holds that power is "merely" a female, a person who's supposed to be inferior. It can be experienced as intolerable humiliation, though it may seldom be expressed or even recognized as such. The more vulnerable the man feels, and the more important invulnerability is to his idea of masculinity, the more he may hate the one he also loves.

Another important contributing factor is that men have society's implied permission to hit their wives or girlfriends. It's probably true that most people would say men shouldn't hit the women they love (or anyone else that they care for or who is smaller and weaker than themselves). But we've seen that historically this idea exists side by side with the traditional assumption that men should be able to control their wives by whatever means necessary. Traditional ideas die hard.

> *"When [men] can't perform up to their standards of masculinity, they may lash out verbally or physically."*

In [a 1974 study conducted by Suzanne Steinmetz and Murray Straus], over half of a sample of husbands indicated they would be jealous if their wives were unfaithful and that they would probably respond with some form of violence. The response of strangers to male violence against women supports the idea that such a reaction is acceptable. Both experimental and real life situations indicate that a woman assaulted by a man in public will not be helped by passersby.

Friends may blame the victim for being in the situation at all, family members may not believe that it's happening and therapists are likely to ask what the woman did to provoke it. Although none of these people state in so many words that they approve of the violence, denial of the battering or the implication that the victim is at fault has the effect of giving the man a "hitting license," especially if the batterer is the victim's husband. He can be quite confident that his friends and family—and perhaps even hers—will stick by him; he probably won't go to jail or even be questioned by police. The social sanctions that keep most of us from acting on violent impulses don't operate in the arena of marriage.

The question of why men batter is often confused with why men become angry at the women they love. A relationship between lovers or family members involves a continual chain of action and reaction, so that it's easy for a man who hits to say it's the woman's sarcasm (or coldness, drinking, poor house-keeping, extravagance) that caused it. Therapists have often taken this view and focused on what the women can do differently to cause change in the men.

Certainly couples trigger feelings in each other, and often they are related simply to expectations, needs and wants at the moment the exchange takes place. They're just as likely to be the result of a history of exchanges between the couple. A man who's had several extramarital affairs will get a different response from his wife when he says he has to work late at the office than will a hard worker whose wife feels confident he's faithful to her.

Displaced Anger

An angry response can also be displaced from a relationship with another person. "You're reacting just like my mother/father/third grade teacher." Or it can be a result of stress. Real world problems like job loss or a sick child can cause tension that easily explodes in anger, given the slightest opportunity. Yet one person's stress is another's challenge; one becomes angry, another depressed and still another works it out in therapy.

Any of these situations can help explain why one person becomes explosively angry and another merely irritated or hurt or worried. None of them explain why one angry person hits his wife, another his child, why one goes out and gets drunk, another verbally lashes out and still another cries or becomes silent and cold or covers up his feelings with jokes. None gives us the answer to why men batter.

Research Findings Are Dubious

Research indicates somewhere around sixty percent of men who batter grew up in homes where they were beaten or they witnessed one parent battering another. However, this is not an explanation either. What about the other forty percent? And what about those who grew up in abusive homes who didn't batter anyone? R. Emerson and Russell Dobash found in a study in Scotland that only twelve percent of the siblings of batterers were violent to anyone. Children model parents' behavior, but they also interpret what they see and connect it with other events, ideas and feelings. It's unpredictable how they'll use what they see and

> *"Denial of the battering or the implication that the victim is at fault has the effect of giving the man a 'hitting license,' especially if the batterer is the victim's husband."*

which parts of it they'll mimic. (This means that if your children have seen their father batter, there is a possibility of helping them interpret the battering in such a way that they won't want to imitate it.)

What makes a man hit the woman he loves is a varied and complicated mix: internal stress; society's permission to hit interpreted as an individual right;

mimicking of violent parents or other role models; interpersonal struggles with the woman and others; feelings of anger, vulnerability, powerlessness and inadequacy; and very few clear actions by the woman, the justice system or others that unequivocally state violence is not allowed.

The Female Role

Women have their image to live up to just as men do. According to the same group of therapists mentioned above, the healthy, mature woman's characteristics are the opposite of the man's: she's very emotional, easily influenced, submissive, excitable, passive, home oriented, unworldly, indecisive and dependent and not at all competitive, adventurous, aggressive, independent or self-confident.

> *"As young women we learn that when we are sexually open, we're subject to severe criticism from parents, men, churches and schools."*

For some women, these characteristics are easier to live up to than those roles men must master. Yet most of us are not easily turned into the marshmallows these traits imply To the extent we're able to be that kind of woman, we can thank the same institutions that mold the male character: the churches that have traditionally tried to suppress women's sexual power and their independence; the school readers that picture girls as hopelessly frightened of spiders and lizards and the dark; the television and magazine ads that show ninety-pound females who do little other than wash and curl their hair, paint their faces and nails and douse themselves with good smells.

The messages, both subtle and direct, inundate us from infancy on ("Isn't she sweet, pretty, tiny, adorable?"). Gradually, we succumb to the idea that we're incapable of making decisions or of acting independently, and that we need protection from major responsibilities as well as from dangerous men. The protector, of course, is that special man in our lives. Many of us are fearful of venturing out at night without male protection and are afraid to live alone. Those of us who work for three or four dollars an hour find it burdensome and depressing to take the entire financial responsibility for ourselves and our children, though many of us must.

As young women we learn that when we are sexually open, we're subject to severe criticism from parents, men, churches and schools. When we assert our independence, show our competence and take responsibility in social interactions men often become angry or hurt and may assume that we're expressing doubts about their ability to handle situations adequately. So when we're at our best—that is, acting openly, independently, competently and responsibly—we face judgments from ourselves and others that are disturbing: "Maybe I'm not a 'real' woman, and maybe my man isn't a 'real' man unless he objects to my independence." Each time we subject ourselves to such a judgment we become less confident and open the door a little bit more to dependency, submissiveness and eventual helplessness.

Why Women Stay

Those of us who manage to rise above the most damaging aspects of sex role socialization to become strong, adventurous, competent people would like to think we're free of male control and violence. But it isn't necessarily so. Although women who have been abused sometimes fit the stereotype of the submissive, dependent, helpless woman, many are the opposite—strong, independent people. They sometimes hold important, demanding, professional positions as doctors, media performers, teachers, or they may work in traditionally male trades. These women have broken out of the restrictive traditional roles, yet are still capable of falling in love, feeling responsible for what happens in an intimate relationship, and committed to going beyond the last mile to make it work.

Every woman learns as she grows up that to be a "whole person" she must have a male partner. Although divorced, single and widowed women constitute more than forty-two percent of the workforce, and though more than sixteen percent of the whole female population never marries at all, the myth persists that every woman must have a man. A single woman may still feel like a freak who accidentally landed on Noah's Ark. Even though men who are widowed or divorced tend to be more depressed and remarry more quickly than women in similar circumstances, most women believe men get along very well without them. This contributes to their placing a low value on themselves and to the fear of never attracting and keeping another man.

> *"Although women who have been abused sometimes fit the stereotype of the submissive, dependent, helpless woman, many are the opposite— strong, independent people."*

Fear of Poverty

The belief that she will be provided for by a man may discourage a woman from taking seriously the need to earn an adequate income. If she does plan a career, discrimination in the job market is likely to make it hard to make a good living. If she leaves paid work for a few years to have children, she's likely to lose both income and self-confidence.

Even a woman who has a good job will suffer a big loss in income when she leaves a man, especially if she has custody of children. The man she's left probably earns much more than she; child support is almost never enough to cover expenses and it's often not paid at all. The fear of poverty or a greatly lowered standard of living is a major reason women stay in abusive situations, hoping year after year it will change and that they won't have to risk making it on their own.

In addition, women still usually take major responsibility for the children, are closer to them and want custody of them, which adds to the financial burden. It may seem impossible to cope with all the children's emotional needs, including the loss of a father figure as well as working full time or more. Although many women do manage to do all that, the reality is, it's a very hard life. Until a woman has done it, and learned firsthand that it's still much less painful than depending on a man who can't be depended on, she'll be too afraid to risk leaving.

Love and Guilt

When an abused woman overcomes her fear of poverty and the pervasive ideas about woman's role and prepares to leave, she may be faced with the abusive man at his most irresistible: "I know I'm a brute, but I'm on my knees asking forgiveness. . . . How could you turn away from me when I most need you. . . . If you really loved me, you'd forgive and trust me. . . . Look how I'm hurting and how hard I'm trying. . . . I'm afraid I'll fall apart without you. . . . You're all I have, all I care about. . . ."

In a few sentences he can trigger the woman's addictive love, her guilt, her concern for him, her feeling that she's responsible for his life and feelings, her hopefulness, her idea that she should be a trusting, nurturing, forgiving woman, and that it would be wrong not to give him another chance, wrong to turn her back on him just as he's finally really ready to change.

She unpacks her bags. The cycle begins again.

Why Men Stay

If a man feels so hostile to his chosen woman that he regularly hits her, why doesn't he leave? If pressed for an explanation, he too might say that it's love that has him locked helplessly in its grip, though he's more likely to mask his feelings with indignant complaints about the woman. He's unlikely to confess that he feels the need of a woman, and that life without an intimate partner would be intolerable. He may not even be willing to admit to himself the importance of the relationship, because emotional dependency runs counter to the accepted image of masculinity.

> *"Many men who batter are immature and emotionally dependent, though some successfully hide it in their work and social lives outside the home."*

Often the man is as dependent on his woman as she is on him, though he may rarely admit it. In their mutual addiction they tend to shut out the rest of the world, she because she's ashamed of her bruises and because he demands that she cut off other relationships; he because he doesn't know how to form relationships and is jealous and fearful of her involvement with others. The more isolated they become, the more dependent they grow, and the more addicted to a relationship they expect to fulfill all their needs. Since no one can fulfill all of another's needs, the continued disappointment leads to increased stress, depression and hostility.

Many men who batter are immature and emotionally dependent, though some successfully hide it in their work and social lives outside the home. They're often addicted to the women they abuse, and they batter in hopes of frightening the women so much that they won't dare "abandon" them. The fear of abandonment often leads to extreme jealousy and to suspicion that a woman will betray her husband with other men, a jealousy often interpreted by both partners as "love."

The batterer believes he can force change by frightening the woman into submission and fidelity, and he, like the woman he victimizes, perpetually renews his hope for change.

Unequal Gender Roles Are Not the Main Cause of Family Violence

by Philip W. Cook

About the author: *Philip W. Cook is a former broadcast journalist who won awards for his reporting from the Associated Press and the Professional Journalism Society.*

Consider this statement: A patriarchal societal structure exists that has as its basis the subjugation of women. Given this structure, women in an abusive relationship have fewer resources than men by which to escape. It is this patriarchy that condones and accepts violence against women. Domestic violence against men should not be placed on a par with domestic violence against women, since the violence against women is a result of a male-dominated society.

This argument is repeated, in one form or another, in virtually all of the books about domestic violence. Historically, one would have had to agree with it. The Napoleonic Code, for example, stated, "Women, like walnut trees, should be beaten every day." Throughout the centuries, women have been buried alive, burned, or tortured for such things as having a miscarriage, even when caused by the husband. It has taken a long time for the "right" of the man to be absolute lord and master in his home to be questioned and to have legal sanctions put against him for battering his wife.

Historically, Men Have Also Suffered Abuse

It is relevant to note that men who suffered battering by their wives were also subject to public humiliation and censures. S. Steinmetz reports this historical background:

> The charivari, a post renaissance custom, was a noisy demonstration intended to shame and humiliate wayward individuals in public. The target was any behavior considered to be a threat to the patriarchal community social order.

Excerpted from Philip W. Cook, *Abused Men: The Hidden Side of Domestic Abuse.* Reprinted by permission of Greenwood Publishing Group, Inc.

Thus in France, a husband who allowed his wife to beat him was made to wear an outlandish outfit, ride backwards around the village on a donkey while holding onto the tail. Beaten husbands among the Britons were strapped to carts and paraded ignominiously through the booing populace. . . . The fate of these men in 18th century Paris was to kiss a large set of ribboned horns.

Certainly, there are many cases in which a woman still must overcome great obstacles in convincing authorities that she is a battered wife. Men also face similar obstacles.

If the patriarchal system is at the root of wife battering, and not other, more important factors such as upbringing, learned behavior, stress, drinking, and lack of conflict resolution skills, then the situations of men and women are very different, and our response to domestic violence—even in today's world—must be different for the genders. Hard data may be lacking, but there are signposts that question this assumption.

Patriarchy + Conservative Religion = Wife Abuse?

"Judeo-Christian doctrine, which espoused the inferiority of women and the supremacy of men, gave its stamp of approval to domestic violence," says *Battered Wives* author Del Martin. Although Martin is speaking of the historical record, the modern assumption is that this is still true.

Merlin Brinkerhoff, Elaine Grandin, and Eugen Lupri used a large-scale Canadian survey of family violence . . . to examine religion, patriarchy, and domestic violence. They report on their findings in the *Journal for the Scientific Study of Religion:*

> Feminists and some social scientists have argued that violence used by men against women in the conjugal relationship reflects male supremacy and a patriarchal order. Much of the rationale for suggesting a relationship between religion and wife abuse stems from the assumption that members of the more fundamentalist groups tend to be more patriarchal. . . . Some people would posit that continued male dominance will lead to increased family violence. . . .

> In the few studies that have explored the role of religious commitment in family violence, church attendance was used as the indicator of religious commitment. The more frequent the attendance, it was assumed, the higher the commitment to the values of the group. . . . Frequent attendance at churches with strong values on patriarchy might actually increase spousal violence. . . .

> The data provide only limited support for this patriarchy thesis; 28.1% of the Conservative Protestants committed violent acts against their intimate partners during the past year. However, contrary to what one might expect from the theoretical rationale, it was not the conservative males but rather the females who were the most abusive toward their mates. Those identifying with no denomination were most violent among males, and were the second most abusive among women and in the sample as a whole. . . .

> *The prediction based on the patriarchy assumption* (i.e., increased violence

with increased attendance) *was not supported.* In fact, the lowest rates of spousal violence were found among those attending church services weekly or more often.

The results of the research concerning church attendance contradict the patriarchy thesis, which suggests that highly committed conservative Protestant males would be the most violent: "To sum up, neither denomination nor attendance seemed to affect spousal violence. . . . The patriarchy thesis, as related to religion, is thus questionable. . . . Other variables, mainly spousal interaction factors, were found to be the best overall predictors of such physical abuse."

Women Versus Women—Where's the Patriarchy?

Another frequently mentioned assumption about domestic violence is that male dominance is a causal factor in producing wife abuse. Stated another way, if society did not condone male dominance, fewer women would be battered. Women who are free of male domestic dominance should then be free of domestic violence.

However, C. Mann's . . . study of females who commit homicide found that 3.4 percent were women who killed their lesbian mates or lovers. *Naming the Violence: Speaking Out about Lesbian Battering,* edited by Kerry Lobel for the National Coalition against Domestic Violence Lesbian Task Force, contains a record of abuse between female partners (unfortunately, the book does not provide any data

> *"The Napoleonic Code . . . stated, 'Women, like walnut trees, should be beaten every day.'"*

about how often such abuse occurs in lesbian relationships). There is ample testimony from the various writers in the book that such abuse does occur and with more frequency than many in the lesbian or battered women's shelter communities acknowledge. Sue Knollenberg, Brenda Douville, and Nancy Hammond of the Task Force on Violence in Lesbian Relationships commented on this phenomenon in *Naming the Violence:*

> Many of us saw the absence of services to lesbians within the battered women's movement as an area needing attention. . . . [A] number of questions surfaced. Did it really happen? Could it be as prevalent as male-female battering? The presence of violence deeply affected our vision of ourselves and our relationships. . . . We were surprised and saddened by the magnitude of the problem and the severity of the violence. . . .

> Many women in the broader battered women's movement are affected by the public acknowledgment of lesbian violence. This acknowledgment forces a deepening of the analysis of sexism and male/female roles as contributors to violence in relationships. To understand violence in lesbian relationships is to challenge and perhaps rework some of these beliefs.

Many of the writers in this book expressed similar views. Another myth that was challenged by informal surveys of lesbian batterers and victims was that the violence was limited only to those influenced by predominantly patriarchal structures into strictly "butch/femme" roles. The surveys and testimony showed otherwise, since feminist lesbians also engaged in domestic violence. Claire Renzetti in her book *Violent Betrayal: Partner Abuse in Lesbian Relationships* finds that lesbians batter each other at about the same rate as couples in heterosexual relationships. Other studies indicate an even higher rate.

Other Studies Question the Patriarchy Thesis

Another significant study in this area was published in the *Journal of Sex Research* and found that 12 percent of gay males studied reported being victims of forced sex by current or most recent partners, and 31 percent of lesbians reported forced sex. It is possible that men are more inclined than women to underreport acts of sexual violence, but the higher than two-to-one ratio of lesbians reporting violent sexual acts by their partners versus gay men counters the common and repeated assertions of domestic violence being the progeny of male patriarchy.

The contributors to *Naming the Violence: Speaking Out about Lesbian Battering* made it clear that they feared the revelations might harm the battered women's movement. This was certainly not their purpose, nor is it the intent of this [viewpoint].

The Causes of Abuse Are More Complex than Patriarchy

The evidence is clear. When we paint with too broad a brush, and assume that every male/female relationship can be blamed on societal structures, we obscure individual circumstances. The most important causal factors for abuse are more complex than patriarchy and are primarily related to circumstances in the family of origin and individuals choosing to be violent.

Violence in the Media Contributes to Family Violence

by David A. Wolfe, Christine Wekerle, and Katreena Scott

About the authors: *David A. Wolfe is a professor of psychology at the University of Western Ontario and a founding member of the Center for Research on Violence Against Women and Children in London, Canada. Christine Wekerle is an assistant professor of psychology at York University. Katreena Scott is completing her Ph.D. in clinical child psychology at the University of Western Ontario.*

It is common knowledge that violence is often glamorized in the adolescent's world, with popular television shows, advertisements, and musical groups presenting violence as a commonplace and acceptable means of dealing with problems. The bombardment of exposure to violent, coercive, and sexist models of relationships (with ample forms of vicarious reinforcement) is coupled with the pressure often put on youths to conform to gender-specific roles as they are seeking to form their own intimate and dating relationships. The media helps this process of confusion along, for example, through attractive portrayals of sex and substance use in television programs and ads. Regrettably, as youth begin to form important personal relationships, many are poorly informed as to how to handle such arousal and competing interests. Such media are not solely responsible for antisocial behavior and gender-based violence, yet they are considered important background influences.

Violence on Television

A look at what many of our children do with their time provides a useful introduction to the ways that violence is socialized into the lives of children and youth. Almost all North American households have at least one TV set. According to the American Psychological Association task force report on television and American society, by the time the average child (that is, a child who watches 2 to 4 hours of television each day) finishes elementary school, he or she will have witnessed at least 8,000 murders and more than 100,000 other acts of violence on television.

Given these numbers, it is not surprising that research over the past three decades has found significant negative effects from viewing TV violence on children's beliefs, knowledge, attitudes and, ultimately, their behavior. In fact, psychological research has led to three prominent effects of seeing violence on television:

- Children may become less sensitive to the pain and suffering of others;

- Children may be more fearful of the world around them;

- Children may be more likely to behave in aggressive or harmful ways toward others.

Violence Becomes Acceptable

It is understandable how children and youth may obtain the idea that violence/abuse is acceptable (or at least normative) among intimate relationships, when they observe the following on TV (based on a substantive review by N. Malamuth & J. Briere, 1986):

- In the vast majority of portrayals of sexual violence, men are the aggressors and women are the victims.

- Sexual violence continues to increase (but remains less common than the portrayal of nonsexual violence).

- Sexual aggression is often depicted quite differently from nonsexual aggression, in that suffering or trauma is often expected of the female victims of sexual violence.

In addition, G. Comstock & H. Paik summarize some of the principal ways in which violence portrayed on television and in movies may heighten the potential influence on children:

- Reward or lack of punishment or consequences for the perpetrators of violence;

- Portrayal of violence as being justified in some way, due to circumstances;

- Portrayal of the perpetrator of violence as someone who is similar to the viewer;

- Portrayal of violence as real events, rather than concocted;

- Portrayal of violent acts that please the viewer.

Media Distorts Reality

In short, television and similar audio-visual media are representative of the manner in which children and youth may be absorbing important messages concerning interpersonal relationships. Regardless of the possible direct effects of viewing violence on television, greater sensitivity is needed in the way in which messages are being provided to children and youth, and how these messages may be distorted in the minds of some individuals to facilitate adversarial beliefs and hostile attitudes toward others.

The social, political, and economic progress made by women over the past 50 years is also reflected in an uneven and distorted manner by the media. A [1990] Canadian Radio-Television and Telecommunications Commission [CRTC] study found that men and women are still depicted differently in almost every area of broadcasting, from programming to advertising, on both radio and television. In television drama, significantly more women are married, interact with children, participate in home management, and have a supervisor at work, whereas significantly more men have paid employment, are in status positions, operate vehicles, and commit acts of physical violence.

Films Present Stereotypical Views

Even more disturbing is the portrayal of sex roles in films. Female actors are stereotypically presented as relatively powerless and passive whereas males are presented as relatively bad, which generates similar sentiments in the individual viewer. These cultural presentations, based on many years of repeated imagery, form a major part of the base of some men's motivation to maintain control and power in a relationship: Women are encouraged to defer to the benevolence of powerful men, and men are encouraged to challenge the autonomy of powerful and assertive women.

"By the time the average child ... finishes elementary school, he or she will have witnessed at least 8,000 murders and more than 100,000 other acts of violence on television."

Stereotypic views of women as submissive and men as being dominant are reinforced by many of the media portrayals of violent and nonviolent acts. Moreover, violence is often modeled and fit into life experiences, so that it becomes commonplace and therefore normative. Not surprisingly, proaggressive attitudes and beliefs are modeled by the aggressors (and sometimes the victims themselves), again reinforcing one's belief that violence is acceptable under certain circumstances.

Children Are Especially Vulnerable

The principal concerns regarding television viewing and children's development were highlighted by a U.S. government task force [in 1982]. Based on two decades of research, the committee concluded that relatively powerless subgroups, such as children and institutionalized individuals, are especially vulnerable to the distorted roles and expectations depicted by television, because they sometimes lack the intellectual and social skills needed to evaluate and resist televised messages. Not surprisingly, they also concluded that the quantity of television viewing was not nearly as important as *what they watch*. For example, the volume of general media consumption has not been shown to correlate with sexual permissiveness, whereas exposure to sexually suggestive materials (such as Music Television and R-rated films), is significantly correlated with premarital sexual permissiveness among youth.

Music Videos

It is particularly noteworthy that both experimental and survey studies show a stronger connection between various attitudinal and behavioral indexes and exposure to music videos *than any other form of media expression.* Rock music has always reflected rebelliousness, and antisocial and sexually provocative images of young people (after all, it is their music). With the advent of rock music videos in 1981, however, the high-impact visual and auditory messages became a powerful marketing success, thus raising questions as to the possible negative influence of such videos. Of concern is the possibility of viewer's *desensitization to violence*, a phenomenon known to occur in other real-world scenarios in which exposure to violence becomes routine or commonplace. Additionally, viewing rock videos has been shown experimentally to have the same effect as viewing pornography: Male subjects express more calloused and antagonistic attitudes toward women.

Clearly, the distortion of gender roles and expectancies is intensified in music videos. According to a 1990 CRTC survey of English language TV, the overall proportion of female characters in music videos is 30%, representing 3% of instrumental players, 19% of singers, and 40% of dancers. We should also be concerned about the way that women are typically portrayed in videos. In a report released by the Quebec Council on the Status of Women, 55% of all rock videos were considered to be sexist (i.e., women were portrayed in submissive or sexually suggestive roles), an increase from 45% in 1988. These distorted portrayals of men and women help to form and reinforce societal stereotypes, and are influential in shaping the normative beliefs of young people about relationships, gender relations, and expectations.

Because such sexist or misogynous portrayals of male-female relationships are relatively common, there is additional concern that some young men will form beliefs that sexually aggressive behavior is sanctioned by society and is not deviant, especially when the victim is an acquaintance. Similarly, there is recent evidence that misogynous rap music, in which musical lyrics express the same negative and sexist attitudes as pornographic material (including the idea that sexual violence is enjoyable for women) facilitates sexually aggressive behavior among college-aged men.

Why Certain Youth Are More Affected

In closing, the question is once again raised concerning those conditions that might make some youth more susceptible to violent or sexist messages while others remain unaffected. Cultivation theory, which argues that TV helps shape viewers' perceptions of social reality, is most germane to an understanding of this process, although TV does not exert a one-way influence—a dynamic, on-going process of interaction between the medium and the viewer seems to best fit the findings.

Using at-risk youths as an example, this theory implies that unsatisfactory conditions in a family promote the affective need for a young person to select and attend to music videos that enable escapism and fantasy. The video may seem more personal and intense than it might to another person from a more satisfactory family environment. For example, J. Strouse [and others] found that girls from dissatisfactory family backgrounds were most vulnerable to the sexually permissive messages of these videos; not only did their attitudes change toward sexual permissiveness, but their endorsement of more permissive sexual behavior changed as well in relation to exposure. Such emotional vulnerability appears to make the minds of these young persons more receptive to the cultivating effect of viewing and listening. As a result, their perception of intimate relationships, sexual involvement, and romance begins to reflect those presented in the video.

> *"Television and similar audio-visual media are representative of the manner in which children and youth may be absorbing important messages concerning interpersonal relationships."*

Men Who Were Abused as Children Are More Likely to Batter Their Wives

by Donald G. Dutton

About the author: *Donald G. Dutton has been researching and working with assaultive men for over twenty years and is the author of several books on domestic violence.*

As a result of my studies, I have found that the biggest childhood contributors to wife assault, in order of importance, are: feeling rejected by one's father, feeling a lack of warmth from one's father, being physically abused by one's father, being verbally abused by one's father, and feeling rejected by one's mother. (I had expected that the relationship with mother would have been the more important, but that wasn't the case.) A cold, absent, and intermittently abusive and shaming father produces a boy with a weak sense of identity (also known as *identity diffusion*).

This is a climate that seems to destroy the soul, a climate wherein the central message is the unworthiness of the self. What if this climate had persisted since birth for these boys? This is not farfetched, for research indicates that much violence begins in early childhood. If the identities of these boys is not nurtured, a stable, positive sense of who they are cannot develop.

The Power of Shame

A father's shaming is the worst thing that can happen to a boy—far worse than simply being reprimanded for misbehavior. Shame is a generalized corrosive punishment of the self rather than a punishment of the act. Being told "You're no good" or "You'll never amount to anything," teaches the child that he is worthless in a way that "I don't like what you did, but I love you all the same" never does. Indeed, anything a father does to imbue a sense of shame has important and lifelong ramifications for his son. Shame is experienced as an attack on the whole self, and shaming incidents are long remembered.

Assailing a youngster in front of others has the terrible effect of public humiliation. The child is overcome with an intolerable discomfort; his very being is open to ridicule by others. As Lenore Terr puts it in her excellent book on childhood trauma, *Too Scared to Cry,* shame comes from "public exposure of one's own vulnerability." Others have defined humiliation as a loss of control over one's identity.

Punishing a child at random is equally pernicious. The boy cannot determine what specifically he has done wrong to deserve the punishment. The effect is to generalize the "wrongness" to the whole self. The shaming aspect of punishment runs deep and conveys a lingering message: that the boy is repulsive, contemptible, and unlovable in a global sense. By obscuring the connection between behavior and castigation, the randomly shaming and punishing father attacks the boy's identity. . . .

Father's Love Is Conditional

In his classic *The Art of Loving,* Eric Fromm describes mother love as "the home we come from, nature, soil, the ocean." All yearning for connection is the longing to return to the perfect, all-embracing love. Father's love, on the other hand, is conditional. Fromm characterizes it as earned or deserved love carrying an unspoken message, "I love you because you fulfill my expectations, because you do your duty, because you are like me." Fatherly love sets limits, punishes, rewards, and judges.

Unfortunately, abusive or rejecting fathers create expectations that are unfulfillable, or they simply up the ante if the child succeeds in meeting their demands. These fathers have a need to punish. In the act of assailing their child, they solidify their own shaky sense of self. And so, the child is doomed. He cannot please, nothing is ever good enough for Papa. The boy feels unlovable to the main source of his male identity. . . .

Some people believe that abusive men will eagerly recount their maltreatment at the hands of their fathers or make up stories as a way of gaining sympathy or exonerating themselves for their current behavior. If that were the case, we would see inflated depictions of terrible early family lives. Yet, in actuality, these men rarely speak of it. Like battered women, they tend to idealize their families and paint rosy pictures of their childhoods that only darken with probing. Their lack of emotional articulateness is startling. What can account for this reticence?

> *"A father's shaming is the worst thing that can happen to a boy—far worse than simply being reprimanded for misbehavior."*

In *When a Child Kills,* lawyer Paul Mones explains that the most difficult cases for him to defend were those in which boys had killed their father or stepfather: The boys didn't want to talk about the abuse they had suffered and would steadfastly defend the parent. This strange loyalty has been likened to the paradoxical bonds that form between hostages and victims in the Stockholm syndrome. It is a survival strategy.

Idealized Parents

Interestingly, our research found that assaultive men whom the courts send to our research and treatment team would also idealize their parents' treatment of them. It wasn't until we mathematically cleansed their self-report questionnaires for *socially desirable responding* (a tendency to deny faults or portray oneself in a positive light) that a closer approximation of the truth came out.

This process of hiding is also true in group therapy. Early in treatment, men euphemize. . . . They describe their fathers as "stern" or "strict." They say, "Dad had a bad temper sometimes," or "He wasn't around much; I guess he liked fishing more," or "The folks did the best they could under the circumstances." Only when I dig deeper and ask specifically, "What did your dad do when he was angry?" or "How did your father show you that he loved you? Can you remember any specific time that he did this?" [does] a more horrifying story emerge.

As a child, the abused boy unconsciously feels ashamed of what goes on in the home but he learns to cover up. He masks his feelings from everyone, including himself. He never invites friends over and secretly envies their home lives. He tries hard to put the shame underground, to bury it. But it never stays hidden. The hellhounds of emotional crisis root it out. Each peccadillo threatens to reopen the chasm of shame. It is for this reason that the boy so relentlessly casts blame outside himself. To accept blame risks too much.

> *"Abusive or rejecting fathers create expectations that are unfulfillable, or they simply up the ante if the child succeeds in meeting their demands."*

Moreover, he is aided and abetted by a socializing culture that for centuries has taught men not to be emotionally expressive—that's only for wimps. The double burden of shame and cultural conditioning makes him retreat to his inner world. Safely ensconced there, he unconsciously begins the task of expunging every possible source of shame from his identity. Men have cosmetically altered everything from a "lower class" accent to racial identity in fleeing shame.

Compensating for Early Wounds

According to his sister, the entertainer Michael Jackson grew up in an abusive home. Each operation he has for his "skin condition" makes him look more white. And Teresa Carpenter's *Esquire* investigation of O.J. Simpson's life tells of his father leaving the family when O.J. was barely more than a toddler. Abandonment is the ultimate rejection, and O.J.'s deepest sources of shame may have included poverty, physical infirmity, and his father's open homosexuality.

As a child, O.J. suffered from rickets and wore braces. Neighborhood kids called him "Pencil Pins." He admitted in an earlier *Playboy* magazine interview that he was "very sensitive" about these taunts. The early wound was there. Then he discovered his escape from early shame; he could run fast with a football. He slowly reinvented himself, erasing his "black" speech patterns and eventually leaving his black wife for a blonde white woman. It would seem that he didn't feel black pride.

> *"As a child, the abused boy unconsciously feels ashamed of what goes on in the home but he learns to cover up."*

Still, the early wounds to the ego wouldn't disappear. O.J. needed constant reaffirmation and adulation in order to know who he was. He felt "alone and lost" on a 1975 vacation in Paris because, in his words, "I was just another tourist who didn't speak the language. Nobody knew me."

Childhood Memories Are Often Blocked

It is not unusual for an abusive man to be unable to recall his childhood. His upbringing is hazy, often with long erasures from his memory tapes. The therapist must piece his past together by asking him probing questions, by interviewing his wife (who usually knows the most), and occasionally by meeting with his mother (who may or may not be forthcoming).

When I started to collect questionnaire data on abusive men I found the same problem with fuzzy memories. Men who initially balk at filling out a scale measuring violence in their family of origin would subsequently turn out to be the ones who suffered the most abuse. They had blanked out or blurred the memories. They would complain to the researcher that they couldn't remember. They would resist filling out the questionnaires. They would repeatedly "forget" to bring them in. They would get angry at the questions asked.

These men were generally more positive about their mothers, although their responses revealed a sense of alternating warm and cold currents. Mother was available at some times; at others, she was cold or angry. (I suspect, although I cannot prove it from my data, that these women were frequently trying to provide maternal support while coping with an abusive husband. It's not surprising to me that they were not always able to succeed.)

The Added Burden of Humiliation

I found that not only had these men been shamed as children, but now, as adults, they are ashamed of that humiliation, heaping shame upon shame. People who have been exposed to shame will do anything to avoid it in the future. They blame others for their behavior. The pain of revisiting the trauma is so great that they have never been remotely willing to examine it. The result is a man who sometimes needs affection but cannot ask for it, is sometimes vulnerable but can't admit it, and is often hurt by some small symbol of lack of love but can only criticize. It is a man who can describe none of these feelings and has forgotten or repressed their source.

The Shame-Prone Personality

Another clue to the nature of these childhood traumatic experiences comes through the work of social psychologist June Tangney. Drawing on earlier work on "humiliated fury" and "the shame-rage spiral," Tangney developed a test in which respondents described which of several reactions they would experience to a variety of everyday mishaps. Tangney differentiated between people whom she called "guilt-prone" and those who were "shame-prone." The former accept blame for a mishap but see it as an isolated mistake.

The shame-prone individual, on the other hand, regards every mishap as indicative of a general flaw in themselves. They cannot make the distinction between a specific mistake and their overarching imperfection. Not surprisingly, this emotional style is accompanied by "hostility, anger arousal, and tendencies to blame others for negative events."

Masking Shame

Shaming creates a vulnerable sense of self, one that can be easily attacked. The shame-prone person feels the first flashes of humiliation at the slightest affront and responds quickly with open rage or humiliated fury. This rage appears so out of proportion precisely because it is being used to prevent *idiocide*, a feeling of death of the self that has already been weakened through earlier attacks. As one of psychiatrist Leon Wurmser's patients put it, "have never been myself except in anger."

The title of Wurmser's book, *The Mask of Shame*, conveys that the exposed, vulnerable self forces one to hide behind a mask. The word *shame* comes from the Old High German root *scama* meaning "to cover oneself." Anger, of course, provides such a mask and externalizing blame protects the individual from having to reexperience the shame. Both are hallmarks of the abusive personality.

In his book *The Seductions of Crime*, UCLA criminologist Jack Katz sees the common underpinning of humiliation and rage. He believes that this accounts for the rapid transformation from the first state to the second. . . .

> *"It is not unusual for an abusive man to be unable to recall his childhood."*

According to Katz, the conversion of humiliation to rage is swift because one is the mirror opposite of the other: Humiliation is the experience of being reduced to a lower position. "In humiliation, one feels incompetent and powerless as if one's stature has been reduced to that of a baby. . . . Humiliation becomes rage when a person senses that the way to resolve the problem . . . is to turn the structure of his humiliation on its head." That is, one puts oneself in a superior position when enraged.

89

Humiliation works from the top of the head down. We blush and then feel a sinking sensation in the abdomen. In contrast, rage proceeds in an upward direction, starting in the belly and working its way up until we "blow our top" or "rise up" in anger.

Shame and the Abusive Personality

Early upbringing plays a major part in formation of the self. At young, vulnerable ages, children are open and susceptible to the vicissitude of family function and dysfunction. The impact of experiences such as violence between parents, angry divorce, rejection, and shaming can take a toll on every part of the child, from his self-concept, to his ability to self-soothe or tolerate aloneness, to his capacity to modulate anger and anxiety, to the elaboration of opiate receptors in the brain, and finally to his compulsive need to externalize blame because accepting responsibility reactivates the mortification.

At every level, from the physiological-neurological to the psychological, the abused/rejected boy is primed to use violence. This is not merely the learning or copying of an action that occurs in violent families, it is the configuration of an entire personality.

"The shame-prone person feels the first flashes of humiliation at the slightest affront and responds quickly with open rage or humiliated fury."

That configuration lays the foundation for the abusive personality. It creates certain pathways, ways of responding that will lead to further reinforcement for abuse: rage with girlfriends, possessiveness, selection of male friends who tolerate or even praise the violent streak.

As the "preabusive" boy enters his teen years, he passes from a latency period, when girls are irrelevant, to a new phase of life with peer groups and messages from the culture and his subculture about what it means to be a man. I believe that abused/rejected boys interpret and accept this information differently, even seek out different information. The message they want to hear is the one that tells them they're all right, that their anger is justified, that women are the problem. As the adolescent moves from failed relationship to failed relationship, he creates a self-fulfilling prophesy filled with fear and loathing that leads him to expect women to be disloyal, untrustworthy, and in need of control.

Hardwired Responses

There is a pool of rage and shame in such an individual that can find no expression—that is, until an intimate relationship occurs, and with it the emotional vulnerability that menaces his equilibrium, the mask he has so carefully crafted over the years. Perhaps it is the mask of a "tough guy," or a "cool guy," or a "gentleman." Whatever identity he had created is irrelevant. Now a woman threatens to go backstage and see him and his shame without the makeup. Then, to his own surprise, the rage starts. He feels it like an irritation, and sometimes like a tidal wave.

He is shocked and surprised. He may apologize and feel shame immediately after, but he can't sustain that emotion; it's too painful, too reminiscent of hurts long buried. So he blames it on her. If it happens repeatedly with more than one woman, he goes from blaming her to blaming "them." His personal shortcomings become rationalized by an evolving misogyny. This misogyny then feeds on itself, contributing further to his rage with women.

At this point the abusiveness is hardwired into the system. The man is programmed for intimate violence. No woman on earth can save him, although some will try.

Elder Abuse Is Caused by Stress on the Caregiver

by Mary J. Quinn and Susan K. Tomita

About the authors: *Registered nurse Mary J. Quinn is the director of probate court services for the California Superior Court in San Francisco. Susan K. Tomita is an associate director of social work at Harborview Medical Center in Seattle.*

Caring for an elderly parent is rapidly becoming a "normative" adulthood life event, and it has been called an "unexpected career." For older persons themselves, care from family and friends is the first choice; care from friends and neighbors is the second choice; and care from formal agencies and organizations is a last resort. Although it may be reassuring to learn that elders are not being abandoned in institutions, family care should not be idealized or romanticized. Some families care for an elder because of their own pathology and their inability to take advantage of formal and informal support. Others are psychologically unable to place a severely impaired elder in a nursing home even though the entire family is severely deprived by the caregiving. And in some instances, caring for the elder involves a search for parental affection and approval, a search that by this time is fruitless. This type of caregiving can be called "excessive caregiving" and may be due to pathology, not heroism or love.

Pressure of Caregiving

There are undeniable pressures on middle-aged children to care for frail elders at home, even though the burdens can be enormous and can extend over a long time. Dementia, which is the most common cause of mental impairment among older people, has a long course, sometimes 7 to 10 years, and the period of total physical care (feeding, bathing, coping with bladder and bowel incontinence) may extend over several years. One study noted that the *average* length of caregiving was 7 years. With time, many physical and mental conditions become even more disabling, requiring higher levels of care. The result is increasing isolation for caregivers, who must focus more and more on meeting the survival needs of the elder and forgo time for themselves. Vacations, a career, education, and friendships may go by the wayside. In a study of support groups for relatives of functionally disabled older adults, feelings of severe isolation and entrapment were reported as the foremost concern. [Another study] found that the heaviness of the burden experienced by the caregivers was directly related to the number of visits from other family members to the household. The more the visits, the less burdened the caregiver felt. Surprisingly, the weight of the burden was *not* related to the level of physical or mental impairment of the elder, or to the duration of the illness, or to behavior problems of the elder.

Additional Stresses

Caregivers are under other stresses too. Frequently, the caregiver—"family"—is one person, usually a middle-aged woman, who does the caregiving with no respite and very little understanding from her spouse, her children, or her family of origin. In fact, her immediate family members may subtly increase their demands on her in order to balance out the attention she is giving to the impaired elder, especially if they do not like the elder. [Tisch] Sommers estimates that 85 percent of caregivers are women. Until the advent of the women's rights movement, it was assumed that middle-class women would stay in the home and care for all dependent members, including the frail elderly. However, this has changed in recent years. Just as women with small children are juggling careers and family, women who have elderly relatives in need of assistance are trying to balance competing demands. The idea of a "Superwoman," who has a career and a family and "does it all," creates pressure and conflict for women of all ages.

Family Pressures

If there is disharmony in the caregiver's family of origin, those family members may feel free to criticize the primary caregiver for the type of help given to the elder, and for the time and money being spent on the elder's care. Old patterns of sibling rivalry can flare up when a parent becomes dependent. Some clinicians have observed an inverse relationship between the amount of complaining done by siblings and the level of contribution they make to the care of the elder: the more complaining, the less contribution. It often happens that the adult child who is doing the most work gets the least credit or is even blamed by the elder,

> *"Until the advent of the women's rights movement, it was assumed that middle-class women would stay in the home and care for . . . the frail elderly."*

while the sibling who does virtually nothing receives praise from the aged person for the slightest contribution. This seems to be true particularly when a daughter is the primary caregiver and the aged parent favors a son who is doing little to contribute to the caregiving. Generally speaking, caregivers receive little or no recognition for the ceaseless work they do. There may be a Mother's Day, but there is no Caregiver's Day.

People who are taking care of their impaired partners, in addition, have to take on household duties that the partner performed previously. The prospect of a life happily shared in old age dissolves as the workload increases. If the partner is demented, there are personality changes which irrevocably alter and diminish the couple's relationship. Some caregivers have noted that they feel as if they are in a state of perpetual mourning for a "lost partner" who is still living.

Gender Differences

M. Fitting and P. Rabins report that there are differences between men and women when it comes to caregiving. They base their findings regarding gender predominantly on spouse caregivers because among studies of adult children as caregivers, few sons were available for inclusion. In a study of 28 male and 28 female caregivers (55 of these caregivers were spouses; 1 was a sister), Fitting, Rabins, and M. Lucas found that there were minimal differences between men and women as to feelings of burden, family environment, psychological adjustment, and social contacts. However, the women had significantly more symptoms of depression than the men. Traditionally, women have had less societal power and therefore have internalized their anger. In contrast, men have had more freedom to act it out.

> *"It often happens that the adult child who is doing the most work gets the least credit or is even blamed by the elder."*

This may account for the overrepresentation of males among reported abusers, given that most caregivers are women.

Interestingly, the men tended to hire help more than the women did, possibly as a result of having been in the world of work and learning the value of delegating tasks. Presumably, men are also more accustomed to having a woman in their lives take care of household tasks and naturally seek to re-create this kind of support for themselves. Younger caregivers were found to resent the caregiving role more than older caregivers, possibly because of other family and career obligations.

Family Roles Affect Caregiver Stress

There is some evidence to indicate that caregiving is experienced differently by partners and adult children. Partners as caregivers often appear to be suffering from greater objective burdens, but adult children have a greater sense of being burdened, possibly because caregiving means more disruption in their lives. Adult children may be more likely to seek physical and emotional distance from their mother or father as time goes on. Partners tend to be more emotionally involved and more distressed by the changes wrought by disease, finding themselves caught up further in the relationship as the dependency deepens. A couple may increasingly withdraw from social involvement as the caregiving needs compound, especially if there is no one to help. If the caregiver's health collapses, immediate institutionalization may result for the impaired spouse. In many instances, adult children will insist on placing their ill parent in an institution when the other parent's health has broken down as a result of caregiving.

> *"A couple may increasingly withdraw from social involvement as the caregiving needs compound, especially if there is no one to help."*

Distinguishing between "normal" aging and changes considered to be treatable pathology has been a challenge to practitioners, researchers, families, and clients. Indeed, recent discoveries showing that much of what has been considered normal aging is in fact pathology have not been publicized sufficiently. This lack of information results in confusion as to whether a given condition is treatable or should be accepted as chronic and inevitable.

Techniques for dealing with disabilities, particularly the behaviors associated with dementia, have not been widely disseminated. Some caregivers feel that if they physically discipline an impaired elder, this will give them control over their problems with the care. They simply do not know what to expect, or which behaviors are not deliberate on the part of the impaired elder.

Obstacles to Caregiving

A caregiver faces many obstacles in trying to provide responsible, competent care: Doctors and other medical practitioners may not offer the desired assistance or information. Caregivers may be too intimidated by physicians to press their concerns. Physicians may not take the time to explain medical conditions adequately, leaving the caregiver with an imperfect understanding of the situation. Community resources such as respite care and in-home services may be sparse in the caregiver's geographic area, or the caregiver may not know how to find or use these resources.

A further difficulty is a lack of adequate role models or mentors for caregivers of the elderly, because widespread longevity is relatively new. It is not uncommon for stressed caregivers to express bewilderment at the quantity and complexity of the work entailed in taking care of a frail elder, wondering aloud, "Why didn't someone tell me?"

Elders as a Source of Stress

The dependent elder himself or herself can be overwhelming for the caregiver. In one study, 63 percent of abusers reported that the elder was a source of stress because of the high level of physical and emotional care required. With demented elders, there are a number of behaviors that can be worrisome and disconcerting for caregivers, such as wandering, primitive eating habits, attacking caregivers physically and verbally, leaving stove burners on, insomnia, and disrobing in public. There is fear that elders will hurt themselves or others. In fact, it is this *emotional* burden, rather than the physical work, that seems to put the greatest strain on caregivers. Doing household tasks, grooming, and transporting an impaired elder are reported by caregivers to be time-consuming but not stressful, whereas the strain of dealing with elders who have emotional problems or severe memory problems creates tension for the caregiver. [Other researchers] note that troublesome behaviors keep the average caregiver in a constant state of vigilance. "Role overload" and "role captivity" were found to be associated with high levels of troublesome behavior, and role captivity intensified when disruptive behaviors worsened. . . .

Other Stressors

Other stressors have to do with the emotional history of the caregiver and the elder. Old battles can come back to life when the elder and the adult child are thrown together. Conflicting ideas about such things as politics, love relationships, raising children, and the conduct of one's work life can arise once again, resulting in renewed anger and resentment on both sides. Character traits which the parent always disliked in the child may provoke "guilt trips." Not all caregivers can control their anger, modulate it, channel it, or understand it. In addition, some parents do not learn to let go of their adult children, failing to perceive them as adults with rights and responsibilities. A parent may berate adult children for what they are not or for what they could have been, or may compare them unfavorably with other siblings. With the onset of dementia, an elderly parent may become disapproving, unable to give the warmth, appreciation, and support that is much needed in the situation. Paranoia may set in, leaving suspicion where once there was respect and regard. The demented elder may become accusatory, putting extra stress on a caregiver already chronically fatigued and doing everything possible to keep the elder comfortable.

Not all older dependent people are abused. The question then becomes: Why some and not others? There are probably two factors other than dependency that must come into play before mistreatment occurs. First, there must be an individual who, for some reason, abuses or fails to take necessary action. Second, there must be a triggering event—a crisis of some sort which precipitates the incident of abuse. It may be that the onset of the elder's impairment or the worsening of health problems creates a crisis leading to the mistreatment, or the mistreatment occurs when the need for assistance exceeds the caregiver's capacity to respond appropriately. Elders may have been fairly independent, but then their need increases, and they turn to an adult child for

> *"A caregiver faces many obstacles in trying to provide responsible, competent care."*

help. Sometimes, parents expect that an adult child will take them in, perhaps in spite of the fact that they have never had an amiable relationship. The elder may see it as the child's obligation, and the child may see it in the same way or may capitulate out of guilt or fear of being judged harshly by friends or family. Some adult children take their elderly impaired parents into their homes too quickly, without considering other viable alternatives or without planning how they will go on with their own lives. The elderly parent and the adult child may have had a good relationship until the dependency began, but the parent's care needs may change the relationship by shifting the balance of power.

Chapter 4

How Can Family Violence Be Reduced?

Chapter Preface

Betty Jean Ashby's life was in danger. She knew it. Her neighbors knew it. Louisville police knew it. The man who was stalking Betty was Carl Branch, her common-law husband and the father of her four children.

When Carl showed up at her apartment on February 10, 1989, Betty climbed out a window, clad only in a shirt, and ran for her life. Carl, wielding an orange crowbar, pursued her across the street and cornered her in the bedroom of a neighbor's apartment.

The neighbor, Marva Anderson, could only hug her four-year-old daughter and cry "Lord Jesus! Lord Jesus!" as Carl hit Betty in the head again and again until she sank to the floor, dead at age 22.

A police officer in her neighborhood had intervened on several occasions in what he called "domestic violence runs." But the officer didn't arrest Carl then and kept no record of Betty's requests for help.

> *Excerpted from journalist Maria Henson's 1990 Pulitzer*
> *Prize–winning editorials in the* Lexington Herald-Leader

As social scientists struggle to find solutions to the problem of family violence, many suggest that the situation faced by Betty Ashby could have been prevented if a mandatory arrest policy had been in place. Proponents of this approach argue that mandatory arrest assures the safety of the victim—not only by physically separating the batterer, but also by discouraging the batterer from future abuse.

However, not all domestic violence situations are as critical as the one faced by Betty Ashby. Opponents of mandatory arrest believe that this policy removes discretion from both the police and the victim in cases where less drastic measures, such as social service intervention or counseling, may be more appropriate. In her work with victims of domestic abuse, academic researcher Janet Mosher finds that "a frequent point made by women survivors of abuse is that they do not want their husbands criminalized. They want the abuse to stop, but they do not want their husbands arrested or incarcerated." Critics of mandatory arrest policies also suggest that arrested batterers may react with greater violence against their victims after they are released.

Mandatory arrest is only one area of debate among researchers looking for solutions to the problem of family violence. The authors in the following chapter discuss the roles that police, physicians, and religious organizations have in helping to reduce family violence.

Stronger Efforts by Police Can Help Reduce Family Violence

by Douglas R. Marvin

About the author: *Douglas R. Marvin is a lieutenant in the New Providence, New Jersey, Police Department.*

While on their honeymoon, 23-year-old Mike becomes verbally abusive to his wife, Mary, after she suggests that he has had enough to drink. Mary is surprised by Mike's behavior and his hostile reaction to her. Soon after, however, he apologizes, and because he has always been so kind and gentle, Mary believes him when he tells her that this will never happen again. Several months later, a similar episode occurs. This time, Mary takes the blame, telling herself that these types of incidents are normal in a new marital relationship. She resolves to do things that will make Mike happy and avert confrontations.

Three weeks later, Mike hits Mary during an argument. After several violent episodes during a 2-month period, Mary finally calls the police because she fears for her safety. Responding officers arrest Mike and charge him with assault under the state's domestic violence laws. Recognizing the trouble that awaits him, and in an effort to get her back on his side, Mike sends Mary flowers while he is in jail. With the flowers, he includes a long note, in which he expresses his deep sorrow for the pain he has caused her and promises that the behavior will never be repeated. Because his note is so compelling, Mary believes that he has learned his lesson and that their relationship will improve. The following day, she informs the city attorney's office that she does not wish to cooperate with the prosecution. When the prosecutor concludes that the state's case is too weak without Mary as a witness, the state drops its charges against Mike, and he is released from jail.

Scenarios such as this have long constituted a staple of American policing. In many communities, reports related to domestic abuse make up the largest cate-

Reprinted from Douglas R. Marvin, "The Dynamics of Domestic Abuse," *Law Enforcement Bulletin*, July 1997. Reprinted by permission of the Federal Bureau of Investigation.

gory of calls to which police officers respond. Yet, until fairly recently, police officers rarely ventured into the private domain of the marital relationship. At most, officers responding to calls for help attempted to calm things down and arrange for one party to leave the home for the evening. While such an approach provided a short-term solution, it rarely helped bring about an end to the violence. During the 1980s, this response began to change as communities implemented more aggressive strategies to address domestic abuse. Many law enforcement agencies began to explore new ways for officers to respond to domestic violence calls. Gradually, the focus shifted from merely "maintaining the peace" to arresting offenders, protecting victims, and referring battered women to shelters and other community resources available to help victims of domestic violence. This move toward fostering a better understanding of domestic violence represents a clear departure from the approach law enforcement agencies once took toward the issue. However, despite the progressive changes that have taken place during the past two decades, law enforcement still does not address domestic violence in the same way it addresses other violent crimes. While investigators attempt to understand the motivations and characteristics of such offenders as rapists or serial murderers, little attention has been given to profiling batterers. Law enforcement officers who must confront batterers on an almost-daily basis would be well served to develop a better understanding of the dynamics of domestic abuse.

> *"Until fairly recently, police officers rarely ventured into the private domain of the marital relationship."*

Officers called upon to respond to and investigate domestic abuse calls need to have a full understanding of the complex social, economic, and psychological issues that surround acts of domestic violence. To assist in the investigation of these cases and to educate police officers about this type of abuse, New Jersey's domestic violence laws require that all police officers receive biannual training in this area. This training brings several pieces of the puzzle together to provide officers with a greater understanding of the dynamics of domestic violence.

Not a Fair Fight

During training, officers learn that domestic violence is not mutual combat. Domestic abuse is about one person dominating and controlling another by force, threats, or physical violence. The long-term effects of domestic violence on victims and children can be profound. A son who witnesses his father abuse his mother is more likely to become a delinquent or batterer himself. A daughter sees abuse as an integral part of a close relationship. Thus, an abusive relationship between father and mother can perpetuate future abusive relationships. Battering in a relationship will not improve on its own. Intervention is essential to stop the reign of terror. When intervention is lacking, the results can be dire:

An average of 1,500 American women are killed each year by husbands, ex-husbands, or boyfriends.

Types of Abuse

Officers investigating domestic violence should have an understanding of the types of abuse they may encounter. Because domestic violence is a pattern of coercive control founded on and supported by violence or the threat of violence, this abuse may take the forms of physical violence, sexual violence, emotional abuse, and/or psychological abuse.

Physical violence includes punching, choking, biting, hitting, hair-pulling, stabbing, shooting, or threats of this type of violence. Sexual violence is characterized by physical attacks of the breast and/or genital area, unwanted touching, rape with objects, and forced sexual relations, including marital rape.

Emotional abuse takes the form of a systematic degrading of the victim's self-worth. This may be accomplished by calling the victim names, making derogatory or demeaning comments, forcing the victim to perform degrading or humiliating acts, threatening to kill the victim or the victim's family, controlling access to money, and acting in other ways that imply that the victim is crazy. Psychological battering involves all of these features of emotional abuse, but also consists of at least one violent episode or attack on the victim to maintain the impending threat of additional assaults. Destruction of property is violence directed at the victim even though no physical contact is made between the batterer and the victim. This includes destroying personal belongings, family heirlooms, or even the family pet. This destruction is purposeful and the psychological impact on the victim may be as devastating as a physical attack.

Characteristics of Batterers

Most batterers are masters of deception. Few exhibit violent behavior to anyone other than their victims. Often, batterers possess winning personalities and are well liked in the community. However, they frequently exhibit vastly different public and personal behavior.

In the wake of a violent domestic abuse incident, batterers often attempt to convince responding police officers that their victims are mentally off balance. Many times they fool officers into leaving without conducting a proper, thorough investigation.

Developing a deeper understanding of the characteristics of batterers will help police officers realize when batterers are attempting to manipulate them. To help identify potential batterers, officers should be aware of other common traits they generally possess. These include:

- Low self-esteem. This often results from physical or sexual abuse and/or disapproval or neglect by a parent or authoritarian figure from the batterer's childhood.
- Extreme insecurity and an inability to trust others. Batterers have difficulty

establishing close friendships. They tend to be critical or jealous of their partners.

- Denial of responsibility for their behavior. Batterers often deny that abuse has occurred. They also minimize the impact of their assaultive behavior or blame their partners for causing an incident.
- Need to control. Batterers choose to abuse their partners. Their purpose is to control them. Batterers use violence or attempted or suggested violence to make their partners comply with their wishes.

The Cycle of Violence

Police generally become involved in a domestic abuse situation once it has reached a flash point. However, in most domestic abuse cases, physical abuse occurs during one of the three phases that make up the cycle of violence. By becoming familiar with the features of each phase in this cycle, responding officers can help victims understand that the cycle of abuse is likely to continue if nothing is done to address the underlying causes.

In a battering relationship, the cycle of violence includes three distinct phases. Investigating officers who understand these phases can offer objective insight to victims of the violence. For example, if an officer can advise a victim that the batterer's next step likely will be to apologize and possibly send flowers in order to keep her in the relationship, she may be more inclined to understand that the cycle will repeat itself if no intervention occurs.

Tension-Building Phase

During the first—and usually the longest—phase of the overall cycle, tension escalates between the couple. Excessive drinking, illness, jealousy, and other factors may lead to name-calling, hostility, and friction. Unless some type of professional intervention occurs at this point, the second phase of the cycle— acute battering—becomes all but inevitable.

During the tension-building phase, a woman may sense that her partner is reacting to her more negatively, that he is on edge and reacts heatedly to any trivial frustration. Many women recognize these signs of impending violence and become more nurturing or compliant or just stay out of the way.

A woman often will accept her partner's building anger as legitimately directed at her. She internalizes what she perceives as her responsibility to keep the situation from exploding. In her mind, if she does her job well, he remains calm. If she fails, the resulting violence is her fault.

Acute Battering Phase

The second phase of the cycle is the explosion of violence. The batterer loses control both physically and emotionally. Many batterers do not want to hurt their partners, only to teach them a lesson and control them. However, this is the stage where the victim, the batterer, or responding officers may be assaulted or killed.

Unless the battering is interrupted, the violence during this phase will take at least as severe a form as is necessary for the abuser to accomplish his goal. Once he has the victim under his control, he may stop. In other cases, where the batterer completely loses emotional and physical control, the consequences can be deadly.

> *"Officers who respond immediately after a violent episode may find an abusive perpetrator who appears extremely calm and rational."*

The violence may be over in a moment or last for several minutes or hours. Although there may be visible injuries, an experienced batterer generally will not leave marks on the victim that would be readily noticeable to others.

After a battering episode, most victims consider themselves lucky that the abuse was not worse, no matter how severe their injuries. They often deny the seriousness of their injuries and refuse to seek medical attention.

Law enforcement officers who respond immediately after a violent episode may find an abusive perpetrator who appears extremely calm and rational. His calm demeanor is deceptive; he has just released his anger and vented his tensions at his victim. The batterer may point to the victim, who may be highly agitated or hysterical because of the abuse, and attempt to blame her for the violence. The victim may, in fact, respond aggressively against officers who attempt to intervene. Officers should be aware that this reaction may be due to the victim's fear that more severe retaliation awaits her if officers arrest the batterer. The victim also may feel desperate about the impending loss of financial support or even emotional support she receives from the abuser. Although officers should not make any false promises, they should reassure the victim that the mechanisms are in place for the criminal justice system to help. Officers have a responsibility to provide a complete, professional investigation so that the system will work. A haphazard investigation, or a lack of concern by responding officers, could result in a violent abuser's being released from jail to retaliate against a vulnerable victim.

Honeymoon Phase

The third phase of the cycle is a period of calm, loving, contrite behavior on the part of the batterer. The batterer may be genuinely sorry for the pain he has caused his partner. He acts out of his greatest fear—that his partner will leave him. He attempts to make up for his brutal behavior and believes that he can control himself and never again hurt the woman he loves.

The victim wants to believe that her partner really can change. She feels responsible, at least in part, for causing the incident, and she feels responsible for her partner's well-being.

It is at this stage that many victims request that complaints against batterers be dropped. If police conducted a thorough investigation, the prosecutor's office can reacquaint a reluctant victim with photographs of her injuries. When the victim sees the cuts and bruises that she received at the hands of her now-apologetic partner, she may reconsider the wisdom of dropping the charges. Likewise, if officers had the victim provide a statement of events at the time of the incident, this could prove an invaluable tool for prosecutors. Not only does such a statement establish probable cause, but prosecutors can have the reluctant victim review the details of her abuse to refresh her memory. Officers and prosecutors also can explain that the contrite behavior being exhibited by the batterer may, in all likelihood, give way to a new cycle of violence. For police officers, the possibility that a victim will forgive her abuser during the honeymoon phase underscores the importance of conducting a thorough investigation. The goal of officers responding to a domestic abuse call should be to develop a case that can be prosecuted even if the victim becomes reluctant.

While most domestic relationships involving violence include some type of cycle, not all violent relationships go through each phase as described above. Some batterers never express any type of remorse for their actions and, in fact, will continue to use threats and intimidation to discourage a victim from filing a complaint or testifying in court. For such abusers, the thought of resorting to flowers or apologies would never cross their minds. However, most domestic abuse cases follow a pattern corresponding, in some way or another, to the cycle of violence.

Future Strategies

In recent years, law enforcement has enhanced its ability to resolve various types of cases by studying the motivations and profiling the characteristics of offenders who perpetrate certain types of crimes. The police can apply this same strategy to help address the issues surrounding domestic violence.

Investigations of domestic violence cases should evolve with a full understanding of the characteristics of batterers and the cycle of violence. Law enforcement officers also should make clear to victims that the criminal justice system can help protect them and will work for their benefit. But the police must back up such guarantees with thorough, professional investigations. The abusive relationships of the past were allowed to persist, in part, because restrictive statutes and misplaced social mores concerning

> *"The goal of officers responding to a domestic abuse call should be to develop a case that can be prosecuted even if the victim becomes reluctant."*

violence within the domestic setting tied the hands of police and prosecutors. Thanks to new laws and an evolving understanding of the dynamics of domestic abuse, these ties have been cut. Law enforcement should make the most of this new freedom to address an old problem.

Religious Leaders Can Help Reduce Domestic Abuse

by K.J. Wilson

About the author: *K.J. Wilson is the director of training at the Austin Center for Battered Women.*

Communities of faith have the potential to be a source of direct and indirect support for battered women. To do so, they must begin to accept their responsibility to prevent, recognize, and intervene in cases of domestic violence. To create an effective response to domestic violence, religious leaders and their congregations must work together to acknowledge the problem, learn more about the issue, work with secular resources, and reach out to the community.

Conduct a Self-Evaluation

Self-evaluation is one of the first steps religious leaders need to take to address the issue of domestic violence. First, to become comfortable with this issue, religious leaders should examine their attitudes, feelings, and beliefs about domestic violence, battered women, and women in general.

Religious leaders must also examine their traditions and theologies to determine whether they are a source of comfort and support for all parishioners or oppressive for some. According to Rita-Lou Clarke, author of *Pastoral Care of Battered Women*, "We need to see that the Bible also speaks of healing for sufferers and forgiveness with repentance and reconciliation. We need to see that divorce can be an option for new life. These views can help to liberate a woman from the bondage of a battering relationship."

Leaders should also evaluate their understanding about domestic violence as well as their strengths and limitations for helping battered women. Many seminaries do not provide instruction regarding ministry in situations of family violence. Some seminarians are not even alerted that they will see family violence in their ministries. One Protestant minister explains that for too many years the need to understand the problem of domestic violence has been overshadowed by the need to maintain the marriage covenant. Religious leaders must begin to understand the dynamics of this issue if they are to effectively respond to battered women and their families. . . .

Acknowledge and Address the Problem

Religious leaders can break the silence surrounding domestic violence by educating congregations about the realities of the issue and, by example, creating an atmosphere in which battered women feel a sense of belonging and support. When religious leaders communicate that it is acceptable to talk about violence in church, they are giving battered women a clear signal that it is safe to ask for help. Once battered women feel safe, they will begin to reach out to others for the comfort and assistance they so desperately need.

"Religious leaders must . . . examine their traditions . . . to determine whether they are a source of comfort and support for all parishioners or oppressive for some."

One way religious leaders can educate their congregations and create a safe environment for abused women is through sermons. . . . In addition, a moment of silence or a candlelight service can be offered for victims of domestic violence, perhaps including testimony from a survivor of domestic violence on a topic such as "How God Helped Me Through My Crisis.". . .

Increase Awareness of Domestic Violence

Religious leaders might also post fliers advertising such local resources as battered women's shelters and adapt curricula dealing with domestic violence for Sunday school classes. Announcements can be made from the pulpit about local shelters and support groups for battered women and abusers. Speakers can be brought in from local shelters or seminaries to speak to youth groups, adult education classes, couples groups, singles groups, social groups, and women's groups in the church. Religious leaders can support observance of National Domestic Violence Awareness Month in October by including relevant articles in the church newsletter. The congregation can supply resources such as money, referral sources, clothes, food, and child care for families in crisis.

Leaders should be alert for signs of abuse among female parishioners, such as frequent church hopping, intermittent attendance, and very private couples who keep to themselves and rarely socialize or interact with church acquaintances or relatives.

The issue of domestic violence can be raised in marriage preparation sessions by questioning couples regarding how they handle disagreements and their families' problem-solving patterns. Leaders can help couples learn how to increase justice and equality in their marriages. They should also be aware that pregnancy is often a time of increased battering for women, a fact that can be addressed in baptismal preparation programs.

Know About and Use Secular Resources

Religious leaders should familiarize themselves with community resources available to battered women, including talking to the local battered women's shelter to learn about the services that are offered. The National Domestic Violence Hotline, (800) 799-SAFE, can provide the names and telephone numbers of community organizations willing to help battered women.

When resources are available, it is advisable to refer battered women or their abusive partners to shelters or batterers' treatment programs. Staff and volunteers of these agencies are trained to deal with abuse and have the knowledge and experience to provide the needed support and advocacy.

A religious leader's wise use of referrals comes from an awareness of his or her limitations and a clear understanding of what his or her role should be. Seldom do religious leaders have the training or time to provide the long-term advocacy that battered women or their abusive partners need. They can often be most effective by serving as support persons and advocates while the battered woman is getting specialized help.

Trust Other Resources

Some leaders are hesitant to utilize secular resources in response to domestic violence. They often do not trust battered women's advocates to be sensitive to the spiritual needs of their parishioners. Likewise, many battered women's advocates are hesitant to trust religious leaders to know how to help battered women. Unfortunately, it is battered women who suffer most from this mutual mistrust. Such resulting lack of cooperation puts them in a position of choosing either battered women's services or pastoral support.

An effective response develops when religious leaders and secular helpers reach out to each other as peers, share information, offer mutual training, serve on boards together, and provide services when referred to by the other. Working together to meet the needs of battered women begins to build the mutual trust that is needed for effective advocacy.

"Some seminarians are not even alerted that they will see family violence in their ministries."

Several years ago Joel Maiorano, a minister at a Christian church in Austin, called me because concerned parents of a battered woman had just contacted him. Although Maiorano had attended the Center for Battered Women's volunteer training class and was knowledgeable about domestic violence, he decided to refer the callers to me. I contacted the concerned family members and was able to provide them with appropriate assistance. By working together, Maiorano and I were able to address the spiritual, emotional, and informational needs of his acquaintances.

Communities of faith can participate in planning a coordinated community response to domestic violence and take the lead in teaching that male violence against women and children is morally wrong. Religious leaders can participate in community activities that discourage violent behavior and support battered women's shelters. Church groups can be encouraged to support local shelters by volunteering and donating money or needed resources. Religious leaders should also encourage the formation of a committee or task force to educate the congregation and recruit volunteers for service.

Mandatory Reporting by Physicians Is Ineffective in Reducing Domestic Violence

by Linda G. Mills

About the author: *Linda G. Mills is an attorney and an associate professor of social welfare and law at UCLA's School of Public Policy and Social Research.*

> I'm sorry, but if my doctor were to call the police and they went to my husband, my husband would have beat the shit out of me.
>
> Anonymous

The arguments in favor of and against mandatory reporting parallel some of the arguments in favor of and against mandatory arrest and prosecution. Health practitioners, like law enforcement and prosecutors, must acknowledge and accept their roles as participants in order for the policy to be effective. The inaction of health care personnel and law enforcement may also have similar negative results.

Identifying Domestic Violence Victims in the Emergency Room

Those in favor of mandatory reporting rely on research that suggests that battered women are much more likely to visit their practitioner than call the police. They argue, and statistics reveal, that battered women are often forced to go to the emergency department or to their primary care physicians seeking medical treatment. These women wouldn't otherwise talk about their domestic violence, and many of them wouldn't otherwise contact the police. Advocates of mandatory reporting believe that it provides an otherwise missed opportunity to hold a batterer accountable for the violence they have inflicted.

Advocates of mandatory reporting policies are particularly concerned about the discrepancy between the percentage of emergency room visits and identification of the cause. In a 1987 study by D. Kurz, in 40% of cases in which the physician treated a battered woman in an emergency department setting, the staff did not discuss the abuse with the patients. Carole Warshaw reviewed emergency room charts at a large public hospital which were generated for women patients during a 2-week period in 1987 and found 52 cases involving women who were deliberately injured by another person (the most obvious cases). Warshaw's results revealed that even though these women gave strong clues about being at risk for abuse, they were only addressed directly in one case "and for the most part, were specifically avoided." In a similar study by W. Goldberg and M. Tomlanovich, only about 4 to 5% of cases of domestic violence were identified correctly by emergency department personnel.

> *"Those in favor of mandatory reporting rely on research that suggests that battered women are much more likely to visit their practitioner than call the police."*

Law enforcement officers who are interested in stopping domestic violence and in holding perpetrators accountable are in favor of mandatory reporting by health care professionals. According to Tim Williams of the Los Angeles Police Department, the mandatory reporting law "helps us get the victim out of harm's way. . . . If there was no Mandatory Reporting Law, we would never know about these things."

Arguments for Mandatory Reporting

Many specific arguments are advanced in favor of mandatory reporting. First, advocates argue that it enhances patient safety by removing the threat to the woman and does so in a way that doesn't require her direct action. Second, they claim that mandatory reporting improves the response of the health care system by requiring it to become involved in patients' lives and to learn the causes of their injuries. Third, advocates support a system of mandatory reporting because it holds the perpetrator accountable for his abusive action. Finally, advocates argue that mandatory reporting improves data collection and documentation of domestic violence incidents, since more women are likely to access the health care system for assistance with their injuries than they are likely to access the criminal justice system.

Blanket Policy Is Ineffective

The problem, as in the case of mandatory arrest and prosecution, is that battered women's lives are too complex for a blanket policy that cannot tailor its response to a victim's unique circumstance. Mandatory reporting by health care personnel is inadequate without additional arrangements for a battered woman to go to a shelter, to seek other living arrangements, or at a minimum, to obtain a restraining order. All too often, she will return home from the doctor or hospital to a batterer who is angry that the police were called. Because of the short amount of time batterers actually spend in jail, they can be arrested in the hospital emergency room and released before the battered woman returns from the hospital. Janet Nudelman of the Family Violence Prevention Fund in San Francisco finds mandatory reporting to be the wrong approach "because it takes away doctors' ability to decide on a case-by-case basis what is best for that patient. It asks them to be cops. It asks them to assume a position that isn't appropriate for them."

Several specific arguments are advanced by opponents of mandatory reporting of domestic violence. The risk of retaliation is real. According to B. Hart, batterers often escalate the violence when their partners either attempt separation or increase their contact with help-seeking organizations. Hart found that as many as half of the batterers in her study threatened retaliatory violence, and more than 30% may inflict further assaults if they are prosecuted. Although it may be argued that battered women benefit from mandatory reporting, insofar as they themselves do not have to take direct action against the batterer, they might still be blamed for having revealed the abuse in the first place.

Other Ways in Which Mandatory Reporting Fails

As [A. Hyman and R. Chez] have argued, reporting has been shown in other arenas, such as elder abuse, to be less effective than education. Moreover, it is unclear whether reporting actually improves the care of battered women. In some cases, especially when intervention by law enforcement has been slow in responding or short in consequences such as jail time, mandatory reporting can actually increase the battered woman's vulnerability to violence. Studies in San Francisco and New York City reveal that in 1991 only 25 to 30% of law enforcement officers prepared the required written reports related to domestic violence calls, and only 7 to 12% resulted in arrests.

In other instances, the reporting can be done by a health practitioner who doesn't truly appreciate the complexity of the battered woman's life and therefore fails to use the intervention in a way that improves her safety. Indeed, an inadequate intervention can send battered women underground as opposed to increasing their access to helping organizations.

> *"Battered women's lives are too complex for a blanket policy that cannot tailor its response to a victim's unique circumstance."*

In addition, some opponents have argued that it is unethical to risk women's lives by imposing mandatory reporting laws in order to collect more accurate data on domestic violence incidents. Some opponents have even argued that the data collected in the confusion of a crisis are inaccurate.

Of particular concern in mandatory reporting cases are the discriminatory attitudes of the mandated reporter: Reporting in child abuse cases reveals that a greater percentage of African American and Latino families are identified as abusive than are white families. In one important study by [S. Cohen, E. De Vos, and E. Newberger], nearly all the health professionals surveyed, most of whom were white, asserted that family violence was a problem associated with people in poverty. Using the example of child abuse reporting, these respondents believed that reporting was necessary only when cases involved the poor. Although some professionals did in fact recognize that child abuse was indicated in their middle class or wealthier private patients, they "did not deem it 'appropriate' to report these cases." Interestingly, even though they believed that the cases involving poor patients should be reported, they often didn't report those incidents as well. Latino, African American, Native American, or Southeast Asian communities were found to have, according to these health professionals, the majority of family violence.

> *"Batterers often escalate the violence when their partners either attempt separation or increase their contact with help-seeking organizations."*

These biased attitudes on the part of health professionals were also detected in their criticism of battered women and were relayed by both male and female health care providers. Battered women were criticized for not following the advice of health care providers. These attitudes were similarly detected in a 1992 study by B. Bokunewicz and L. Copel of emergency nurses' attitudes about domestic violence. The researchers found that stereotypes about battered women were common: beliefs such as that the battered woman could leave or was masochistic or that the violence was a one-time incident were prevalent. Despite the fact that D. Kurz found that 75% of battered women volunteered that they had been injured by a husband or boyfriend, emergency department staff still stereotyped battered women as "evasive" or as possessing "troublesome" traits, or both.

Doctors Reluctant to Get Involved

Doctors themselves are sometimes uncooperative because they fear that by reporting they will make the situation worse. Dr. Larry Bedard, President of the American College of Emergency Physicians, was quoted as saying "I feel a lot of trepidation when I am faced with a situation where a woman says, 'Please don't report, because if you do, my husband will kill me.'"

The refusal of doctors "to get involved" in cases of domestic violence may have criminal or fiscal consequences. In some states, such as California, non-compliance with domestic violence reporting laws is a misdemeanor. In addition, battered women have started to hold doctors liable for their inaction, in much the same way they held police agencies liable. Tort law in this area is still evolving; for now, physicians can be held liable under civil law for failing to report abuse to the police. The issue is particularly thorny because it involves an adult, not a child, an elder, or a dependent or "incompetent" adult. In child, elder, or dependent adult abuse cases, liability is clearer when the cases involve people who aren't otherwise competent to protect themselves. The threat of money damages can be a powerful incentive for physicians to act, while also compensating the victim financially for her injuries.

Physicians Avoid Inquiring About Abuse

Mandatory reporting, of course, relies on the interest of the health care professional. Health personnel have been extremely reluctant to ask how a victim sustained an injury, avoiding the problem of reporting by avoiding the relevant inquiry. In one study by S. Reid and M. Glasser, it was found that physicians failed to identify the majority of domestic violence victims, even though they were often the first and only individuals to whom the victim presented. The study assessed a total of 143 primary care physicians in three midwestern counties to determine the physicians' knowledge of and attitudes toward domestic violence, the importance and prevalence in their practice of intimate abuse, and their attitudes toward responsibility. In addition, the study collected information on current practices and protocols, level of education on domestic violence received, and opinions on how best to distribute information concerning domestic violence. . . . Their results revealed that 100% of the physicians agreed that finding and treating domestic violence was important, yet less than half agreed that domestic violence was a significant problem in their patient populations. Almost 96% of the physicians surveyed believed that more should be done to educate physicians about domestic violence. Indeed, 94% agreed that domestic violence should be included in a doctor's professional medical training. Yet, nearly half of those surveyed reported that they would not participate in a domestic violence forum. Although 41% reported that they had received some formal education regarding domestic violence, 57% felt that their medical school education had not prepared them to deal with the issues related to domestic violence. Less than 25% reported that they had been trained to diagnose domestic violence. In total, family and female physicians were more comfortable addressing issues related to domestic violence, whereas older physicians were less comfortable and less likely to agree that education about domestic violence should be a part of medical training.

> *"Of particular concern in mandatory reporting cases are the discriminatory attitudes of the mandated reporter."*

Other Health Care Professionals Also Reluctant

Another study that included dentists and dental hygienists revealed some very interesting and disturbing results. Compared with physicians, psychologists and social workers, dentists and dental hygienists received the least education in abuse and had the least frequent rate of suspecting abuse and the greatest proportion of respondents who felt they were not responsible for intervening in suspected abuse. In total, 45.9% of the dental hygienists and 47.3% of the dentists did not agree with the statement: "Professionals in my discipline have as much responsibility to deal with problems of family violence as they do to deal with other clinical problems." This finding is particularly striking when one contemplates that so many domestic violence incidents involve the face (68%), the eyes (45%), and the neck (12%).

In another study, it was confirmed that health professionals were reluctant to ask the questions that would trigger a reporting situation. C. Allert, C. Chalkley, J. Whitney, and A. Librett reported the results of domestic violence training provided to health care professionals in Utah. Included in the training were Emergency Medical Technicians and paramedics, as well as emergency department personnel. The trainers and researchers found that, although providers felt confident asking questions about abuse, the providers were unwilling to question patients unless they suspected domestic violence was the cause of the injury. The reason, according to [researchers], is that these providers did not believe domestic violence was a problem in their communities.

In one study of five communities, the researchers examined how domestic violence had been integrated into the health care system. It was found that charismatic leaders were the people responsible for inspiring change in how a health care organization addressed domestic violence but that those leaders often found themselves marginalized in the health care setting and without resources for ensuring the program's ongoing success. When the charismatic leader left, the domestic violence program usually fell apart.

Few Programs Are Successful

Occasionally, program advocates are successful in fully integrating a domestic violence agenda into a hospital setting. WomanKind is one of the oldest hospital-based programs and is located in two suburban hospitals and one urban hospital in the Minneapolis-St. Paul area. With an annual budget of $200,000, a director, four full-time program coordinators, and 75 volunteers, WomanKind trains hospital staff to identify and respond to domestic violence. Crisis intervention for victims and ongoing support during and after their hospital stay is available, as is access to other resources, including safe housing, legal aid, and welfare.

These findings suggest that despite the various forms of mandatory reporting laws, physicians' reluctance must be overcome if the goal is to involve the health care system in domestic violence intervention. This limitation aside, it is highly questionable whether mandatory reporting actually serves the complex and highly individualized interests of most battered women who need services.

Mandatory Arrest and Restraining Orders Are Ineffective

by Richard L. Davis

About the author: *Richard L. Davis is a professor of sociology at Quincy College in Plymouth, Massachusetts. He is also a retired police lieutenant.*

> To become properly acquainted with a truth we must first have disbelieved it, and disputed against it.
>
> Otto von Bismarck (1815–1898)

It is said that for every complex problem there is a simple and elegant solution that is wrong. I believe that our public policymakers love easy solutions. "Indians on good land? Move 'em out. You want Texas? Start a war with Mexico. Crime problem? Bring back the death penalty. Prayer in schools will solve the moral lapse of the nation. Busing schoolchildren will end racial segregation. Problems with domestic violence in our homes? Make a law that will forbid it. Those who have been abused and are afraid of the abuser? Make a law that states we will arrest the abuser and then promise the victim that we will protect her. Have you got any other problems you want us to solve?"

Mandatory Arrest and Restraining Orders Are Ineffective When Used Alone

Mandatory arrest and the use of civil restraining orders without proper criminal sanctions are assuredly flawed solutions for preventing the complex enigma of domestic violence. Americans have historically objected to the government's attempt to legislate what they consider their private morality or family problems. Prohibition was a colossal failure, and the government's policies concerning abortion appease almost no one. Only when arrest policies are coordinated with valid intensive probation, judicial sanctions for chronic abusers, and substantial and intensive community supervision by community domestic violence

Excerpted from Richard L. Davis, *Domestic Violence: Facts and Fallacies*. Reprinted by permission of Greenwood Publishing Group, Inc.

services coupled with early intervention educational programs in our schools will we begin to have progress.

The use of civil domestic violence abuse prevention orders, mandatory arrest of violators of those orders by police policy, and de facto mandatory arrest by preferred arrest policies for domestic violence are most often not followed with proper criminal sanction by the courts. In most of the states that have preferred arrest policies, because of the fear of lawsuits by police departments and the inability of nearly anyone to understand just what is meant by "preferred arrest," police departments often require their officers to arrest someone in almost all domestic violence incidents.

Mandatory Policies Remove Police Discretion

The Abuse Prevention Order, commonly referred to as a restraining order, attempts to prohibit an abuser from further abusing the victim of domestic violence by issuing a civil protection order that demands the abuser vacate the home, stay away from both the home and the plaintiff, and have no contact of any kind with the plaintiff or the plaintiff's children. Under current Massachusetts law, similar to many other laws nationwide, a police officer who has probable cause to believe that a criminal provision of a domestic abuse restraining order has been violated is *mandated* to arrest the abuser even though the act is a misdemeanor. The criminally enforceable provisions of restraining orders are only those sections to vacate, stay away, and to have no contact with the plaintiff or the plaintiff's children.

"Mandated arrest . . . is unique in that a police officer is provided with no discretion to determine whether or not to make an arrest."

This mandated arrest provision is unique in that a police officer is provided with no discretion to determine whether or not to make an arrest. This impugns the tradition of victim preference and officer discretion to respond to the desire and concerns of the victim that has long been recognized and generally accepted as an important role in determining proper police action. Mandatory arrest, and hence disregard of the victim's desire may also reinforce the belief of many women that the patriarchal institution of state government is still "Big Brother" and not "Big Sister." The law implies that women, at least some women, are incapable of making rational decisions on their own.

Studies Do Not Support Mandatory Policies

The only empirical scientific study to date that examines the complex but important relationship of mandatory arrest and domestic violence in Massachusetts concludes that, while arrest rates increased, the injury rates of victims and the number of domestic violence calls to police did not decrease. That same report proclaims: "The findings of Sherman and Berk in Minneapolis encouraged arrest in cases of domestic violence." What the report does not announce is that the Minneapolis study *does not* encourage the arrest of all suspects of domestic violence incidents. The experiment contained cases in which police were *empowered* to make arrests. In the second paragraph, of the first page, Sherman and Berk determine that "It may be premature to conclude that arrest is always the best way for police to handle domestic violence, or that all suspects in such situations should be arrested. A number of factors suggest a cautious interpretation of the finding."

> *"[Mandatory arrest] law implies that women . . . are incapable of making rational decisions on their own."*

The Massachusetts study omits that Sherman and Berk do not prefer mandatory arrest laws. In fact, Professor Sherman has written that Massachusetts, by passing "mandatory arrest" laws for misdemeanor domestic violence violations, has not helped but rather has compounded the problem. Sherman's report is resolute in its finding that mandatory arrest laws are unwise and should be repealed. Professor Berk is not as certain, yet he concludes, "A better policy than simple mandatory arrest for all offenders, regardless of risk category, would be to couple an arrest for high risk offenders with additional measures to protect victims."

No study nationwide has produced any empirical scientific evidence that mandatory arrest laws have been effective in reducing the number of assaults and abuse calls. Such calls to police departments, both in Massachusetts and nationwide, continue to increase. The Massachusetts Trial Court operates a Judicial Response System, a statewide emergency program designed to assist law enforcement in resolving emergency legal situations by providing the services of a judge by phone when court is closed. In fiscal year 1985, 324 calls were placed; in fiscal year 1994, 14,878 calls were placed. Requests for restraining orders accounted for 13,374 of the total.

Other Studies Are Ignored

After the Minneapolis study and with support from the National Institute of Justice, further studies were conducted in Omaha, Nebraska; Charlotte, North Carolina; Milwaukee, Wisconsin; Metro-Dade (Miami), Florida; and Colorado Springs, Colorado. A study in Atlanta, Georgia, was funded, but to date no results have been published. Interestingly, I placed many calls to the National Institute of Justice and could not locate anyone who knew anything about the Georgia project. When the findings of these studies were released, the results were mixed. In general, the studies showed that arrest by itself may not be the primary factor in modifying future violent behavior. Those involved in the studies were not invited to appear on a series of television shows, as was Professor Sherman after the original Minneapolis study. *In fact, these studies seem to*

*have been universally ignored by public policymakers, women, and victims'
right advocates.* In an even more bewildering development, the results from
most of these followup studies, which for the most part did not substantiate the
outcome of the Minneapolis study, were vilified and criticized by the *very
people* who enthusiastically supported the conclusions reached by the Minneapolis study.

The Case for Mandatory Arrest Is Challenged

Some of these latest studies contain results that are complex but challenge the
central premise that arrest works best in all domestic violence circumstances.
Some of these most recent studies produced evidence that in some cases arrest
would *increase* the frequency of future domestic violence. In Milwaukee, Omaha, and Colorado Springs, results from the studies demonstrated that those
who were unmarried or unemployed and were arrested because of domestic violence became even more violent after the arrest. Among married and employed suspects, arrest did have a deterrent effect. Arrest results vary from city
to city and from individual to individual. A summary of these studies to date indicates the following,

- Arrest reduced domestic violence in some studies but increased it in others.
  Milwaukee, Charlotte, and Omaha produced evidence that arrest *increased
  violence* in some cases. Colorado Springs and Metro-Dade reported that the
  risk of further violence was reduced.
- Arrest reduces domestic violence among employed people but increases it
  among unemployed people who often believe they have nothing to lose.
- Arrest reduces domestic violence in the short run but escalates violence
  later in older and distressed urban cities.
- A small but chronic portion of all violent couples produces the majority of
  domestic violence incidents.
- Many offenders who flee before police arrive are substantially deterred
  from future violence by warrants for their arrest.
- Police, because of prior calls for service, can determine which couples are most likely to suffer future violence.

These results suggest that arrest alone is not consistently the correct

*"No study nationwide has
produced any empirical
scientific evidence that
mandatory arrest laws
have been effective."*

course of action. All intervention cannot and should not be by mandatory arrest
policies or civil restraining order. In these studies, the majority of those arrested
were released within a few hours, and only a small number were held
overnight. The legal sanctions were limited to the arrest process. For sanctions
to be effective, some sure, equitable and swift discipline or punishment must
come from the actions of prosecutors and judges whose job is supposed to mete

out sanctions when and if the abuser is found guilty.

Results from a study released in January 1991 reveal that almost half of the female victims who reported they were victims of intimate violence said that violence was a private or personal matter and they did not report it to the police. Schools, separate treatment programs for both perpetrator and victim, shelters, and other community intervention and education may better assist some of these perpetrators, particularly those who are not chronic criminal offenders, and many of the victims.

No Data Supports Mandatory Arrest

I have found no studies or data to provide any credible reason for mandatory arrest policies, particularly without proper sanctions anywhere in the criminal justice system. Logic alone should lead us to conclude that, if mandatory arrest policies deterred criminal behavior, the same policies would be used in drunk driving, drug interdiction, and child abuse. Some of these crimes include mandatory sentencing policies but not mandatory arrest policies. . . .

> *"Recent studies [have] produced evidence that in some cases arrest would* increase *the frequency of future domestic violence."*

Nowhere is there a carefully documented, well-organized, original, and convincing body of evidence that mandatory arrest has caused any change in criminal behavior. . . . The conclusion I have reached, along with many others I have worked with in the criminal justice system, is that these procedures are just highly visible, inexpensive attempts by public policymakers to persuade women's and victims' rights advocates and battered women's groups that they, the public policymakers, are doing *something/anything* to combat domestic violence.

Policymakers Are Misguided

The police and court logs that are printed in many of this nation's daily and weekly newspapers can provide a carefully documented, well-organized, original, and convincing body of evidence that much of our current domestic violence policy remains as follows: "have the police arrest the abuser, have the court system let them go." What we are left with is the familiar refrain of "arrest them, let them go, arrest them, let them go." That is the only real *something/anything* that public policymakers have given us to combat domestic violence.

Many public policymakers and some practitioners in the criminal justice system believe that women will be safer once they have been separated from their abuser. The truth is that, in Massachusetts, mandatory arrest policy or not, the abuser is most often legally separated from the victim for only a matter of hours when arrested by the police. Quite frequently, there is evidence that the violence inflicted after separation of the couple can be substantial, in fact, in certain circumstances violence may even escalate. It is a fact that, "75 percent of spousal murders happen after the women leave."

Even though no major study has been done on the effectiveness of civil protection orders concerning their effect in reducing spousal domestic violence and there is a complete absence of any scientific empirical data on the efficacy of these orders, they are now available in fifty states. Both Peter Finn and Sarah Colson are aware of the lack of any credible or convincing evidence that demonstrated that restraining orders could effect violence recidivism when they wrote that "Properly used and enforced, protection orders can help prevent specific behaviors such as harassment or threats which could lead to future violence. They also can help provide a safe location for the victim, if necessary, by barring or evicting an offender from the household, and establish safe conditions for any future interactions, for supervised child visitation.

> *"[Research study] results suggest that arrest alone is not consistently the correct course of action."*

A restraining order may be effective to deter the rational, reasonable, and stable person who is not likely to and has no history of acting out in a violent manner. If a person is rational, reasonable, and stable there should be little real need of a restraining order. With this segment of the population and properly implemented, restraining orders may prove to be effective. This is not, however, the person that law enforcement frequently has as a client.

Other than the eviction process, which is almost always accomplished with the aid of the police, Finn and Colson readily concede that they know of no scholarly apparatus, scientific study, or empirical data showing any evidence of what they conclude will be or has been accomplished. This lack of scientific study or empirical evidence did not stop Finn and Colson from being confident about achieving the proper results. Am I missing something here?

Doing More Harm than Good

If empirical data from the National Institute of Justice studies demonstrate that the issuance of these orders in Massachusetts and elsewhere can *encourage rather than deter acts of violence,* as some of the studies have demonstrated, who will take responsibility for precipitating the violent actions of the abuser because of the issuance of the order? Are we to continue to believe that it is always better to do something rather than nothing? Am I wrong to question the wisdom of issuing a domestic violence protection order if there is data that under certain circumstances the issuance of a domestic violence protection order may actually be the catalyst of further violence?

Religious Communities May Exacerbate the Problem of Child Abuse

by Shauna Van Praagh

About the author: *Shauna Van Praagh was a Boulton Fellow at the Faculty of Law of McGill University. She has taught at the law faculties of Columbia University, King's College London, and McGill.*

The teachings of a religious community with respect to children may be translated into parental practice, and therefore become central to a child's day-to-day life. And yet, while religions concern themselves with doctrine relating to the rearing of children, children do not choose to be members subject to that doctrine. Child membership in religious communities, in fact, is unique in that it is not based on any notion of the free choice to join or not join. . . . At the same time, child membership is crucial to the continuation of religious communities, and, . . . it is generally enforced through the liberal mechanism of individual freedom of religion held by parents.

The Religious Community's Power over Children

The power structure of the religious community and its relationship to children thus becomes clear: the membership level represented by children is one without power as compared to those levels represented by adults (of course, women and men usually represent different power levels). Indeed the community has a vested interest in exerting power over its child members. This observation takes nothing away from the notion that children may develop their identities partially within their religious community . . . ; nor does it deny that the community may be nurturing and supportive, educational, and significant to a child's sense of self. Yet it does suggest that the considerable control that a religious community may exert over the life of a child, whether or not through parental practices, carries with it negative potential. The same connections that

Excerpted from Shauna Van Praagh, "The Youngest Members: Harm to Children and the Role of Religious Communities," in *The Public Nature of Private Violence: The Discovery of Domestic Abuse*, edited by Martha Albertson Fineman and Roxanne Mykituk. Reproduced by permission of Taylor & Francis/Routledge, Inc., http://www.routledge-ny.com.

[are] worthy of protection in a child's life may need to be readjusted or indeed severed if they result in severe harm to that child.

The Religious Community and Abuse

Child abuse, or violent harm directed at children, can be connected to religious communities in three general ways. First, the insularity of the community, in protecting members from outside observance or scrutiny, may shield children from needed help. The case of Yaakov Riegler, widely reported in 1992, might be read as an example. Yaakov, an eight-year-old mentally retarded boy whose family belonged to an insular Orthodox Jewish community in Brooklyn, was beaten to death by his mother, four years after the New York City child welfare system had first learned about abuse in the Riegler family. While the harm can-

> *"The [religious] community has a vested interest in exerting power over its child members."*

not be said to be directly correlated to religiosity or religious values in this type of case, the way of life of the community might indeed serve as a barrier to remedies available on the outside. In another much-publicized example, and one where the connection between child and religious community is even clearer, given the absence of parents, the cases of children sexually abused in Catholic orphanages focus on the possible insularity associated with domestic life.

Punishing Children for Nonconformity

Second, the community may require punishment for failure to conform to its norms or standards—or, at least, parent members of the community may understand their obligations to include punishment of children who do not obey the tenets of their religion. As an example, we need only turn to the *Child, Family and State* casebook widely used in law school courses dealing with children and law, to find the following problem:

> Eleanor Papillon is a 20-year-old single parent. She is a devoted member of a fundamentalist religious sect, one of the tenets of which is to strongly disapprove nonmarital sex. Eleanor's son Danny is four years old. When Eleanor took Danny in for an annual medical checkup, the pediatrician—Dr. Thomas Stein—noticed that Danny had bruise marks on his arms, stomach, back and buttocks. The doctor asked Eleanor what had happened. Eleanor said that during a visit to his aunt's house three days before, Danny had been discovered under a bed with his pants off with a little girl, also aged four, who had her pants off. Eleanor reported that she had beaten Danny that night at home, after she became enraged by his refusal to admit what he had done.

Introduced to provoke a discussion of the tension generated by the parental privilege to use corporal punishment, the social interest in child protection, and the value of family privacy, the problem also raises the difficult issue of the interaction between the norms of the group to which the mother belongs and the norms of the state. If we stretch the domestic sphere in the way suggested above, the religious community can also be seen to play a role in what looks like excessive physical punishment. In a more drastic example (and one where the community is understood as cultural rather than strictly religious), the parents of Tina Isa, a sixteen-year-old girl whose job at a fast-food restaurant and desire to take part in high school social events clashed with traditional Palestinian culture, were found guilty of murdering their daughter after attempts to control her activities failed.

Religious Teachings May Encourage Abuse

Third, and most difficult to confront, the teachings and practices of the religion itself may harm children. They may endorse severe physical or even sexual abuse, they might be understood to result in serious emotional or psychological harm, or they may prevent access to necessary care. As the reader will no doubt note, difficulties in definition immediately arise with respect to this assertion. Obviously, the state—including child welfare officials and courts—may invest in a concept of harm different from that held by the religious communities in question. In labeling *abusive* certain behavior, mandated or at least supported by religious norms, the law interferes dramatically with the community itself, and aggressively severs the bonds between child and religious community.

A particularly striking example in the realm of "strong discipline" crossing into physical abuse is that of a Montana case *(State v. Riley)* in which members of the River of Life Tabernacle acted according to their religious tenets in beating a young child with a fiberglass stick and forcing him to stand for long periods of time in cold mud. The child died as a result, and members of the community were convicted of homicide. Indeed, as argued by [researcher] Philip Greven, contemporary fundamentalist Protestant doctrine on child-rearing in general is informed by the themes of submission and suffering, and in turn teaches that God requires spanking, discipline, the use of the rod, and the breaking of children's independent wills:

> *"The insularity of the [religious] community ... may shield children from needed help."*

> Anglo-American Protestants have always been among the most vocal public defenders of physical punishment for infants, children and adolescents. They have provided many generations of listeners and readers with a series of theological and moral justifications for painful blows inflicted by adults upon the bodies, spirits, and wills of children. These defenses remain crucial to any understanding of the earliest sources of suffering and violence in our lives and culture. It is no accident that the shelves of evangelical and fundamentalist Protestant bookstores throughout the land are filled with books advocating physical punishments as the "Christian" method of discipline, essential to the

creation of morality, spirituality, and character, and vital, ultimately, to the salvation of souls.

From the religious community's point of view, of course, these actions are believed to serve the interests of the children involved, both in this world and in that to come. And yet, if we refer to the work and analysis of Alice Miller, as does Greven, we might worry about the destructive consequences—including anxiety, fear, hate, depression, dissociation, sadomasochism, domestic violence, aggression, and delinquency—that have been attributed to the physical punishment of children.

Faith Healing as Abuse

In a context different from abusive punishment, but one in which the clash in child-rearing norms between specific religious communities and the state is particularly marked, adherence to the notion of faith healing can have a negative or even fatal impact on the life and health of children. Statutory exemptions from child abuse and neglect statutes for parents who rely solely upon spiritual healing are currently being questioned, and Christian Science parents whose children have died as a result of lack of medical care have been prosecuted in several states. From the perspective of the community, the law's reaction to its principles constitutes a severe attack on its relationship with member children. Indeed, a recent case found the Christian Science Church liable for the wrongful death of a member's son who received no medical treatment for meningitis, and thus targeted the community *per se* rather than the individual parents of the child.

Law Enforcement Must Be Willing to Intervene

The very suggestion that harm to children might be connected to the religious communities to which they belong requires a distancing from the perspective of the communities themselves. While the possibility of such harm does not weaken the notion that religious communities may play a significant role in the lives of children, it does raise substantive questions as to the nature of that role. Enlarging the "domestic sphere" through the addition of religious community, then, does not insulate the relationship between community and children from scrutiny. But it does mean that the law, in intervening to protect children's interests, needs to justify its readiness to cross into that sphere and disrupt the relationship.

Bibliography

Books

Ola W. Barnett et al.	*Family Violence Across the Lifespan: An Introduction.* Thousand Oaks, CA: Sage Publications, 1997.
Raquel K. Bergen, ed.	*Issues in Intimate Violence.* Thousand Oaks, CA: Sage Publications, 1998.
R.C. Bird	*Domestic Violence and Protection from Harassment: The New Law.* Bristol, England: Family Law, 1997.
Kevin Browne and Martin Herbert	*Preventing Family Violence.* New York: Wiley, 1997.
Patricia J. Brownell	*Family Crimes Against the Elderly: Elder Abuse and the Criminal Justice System.* New York: Garland, 1998.
Ricardo Carrillo and Jerry Tello, eds.	*Family Violence and Men of Color: Healing the Wounded Male Spirit.* New York: Springer, 1998.
L.B. Cebik, Glenn C. Graber, and Frank H. Marsh, eds.	*Violence, Neglect, and the Elderly.* Greenwich, CT: JAI Press, 1996.
Elaine P. Congress, ed.	*Multicultural Perspectives in Working with Families.* New York: Springer, 1997.
Charles P. Ewing	*Fatal Families: The Dynamics of Intrafamilial Homicide.* Thousand Oaks, CA: Sage Publications, 1997.
Richard J. Gelles	*Intimate Violence in Families.* Thousand Oaks, CA: Sage Publications, 1997.
L. Kevin Hamberger and Claire Renzetti, eds.	*Domestic Partner Abuse.* New York: Springer, 1996.
Sharon D. Herzberger	*Violence Within the Family: Social Psychological Perspectives.* Madison, WI: Brown and Benchmark, 1996.
Carolyn Hoyle	*Negotiating Domestic Violence: Police, Criminal Justice, and Victims.* New York: Oxford University Press, 1998.
Valerie Jackson	*Racism and Child Protection: The Black Experience of Child Sexual Abuse.* New York: Cassell, 1996.

Bibliography

Rafael A. Javier, William G. Herron, and Andrea J. Bergman, eds. — *Domestic Violence: Assessment and Treatment*. Northvale, NJ: J. Aronson, 1996.

Tanya F. Johnson, ed. — *Elder Mistreatment: Ethical Issues, Dilemmas, and Decisions*. New York: Haworth Press, 1995.

Suman Kakar — *Domestic Abuse: Public Policy/Criminal Justice Approaches Towards Child, Spousal and Elderly Abuse*. San Francisco: Austin and Winfield, 1998.

Seth C. Kalichman — *Mandated Reporting of Suspected Child Abuse: Ethics, Law, and Policy*. Washington, DC: American Psychological Association, 1999.

Glenda K. Kantor and Jana L. Jasinski, eds. — *Out of the Darkness: Contemporary Perspectives on Family Violence*. Thousand Oaks, CA: Sage Publications, 1997.

Javad H. Kashani and Wesley D. Allan — *The Impact of Family Violence on Children and Adolescents*. Thousand Oaks, CA: Sage Publications, 1998.

Susan L. Keilitz et al. — *Civil Protection Orders: The Benefits and Limitations for Victims of Domestic Violence*. Williamsburg, VA: National Center for State Courts, 1997.

Alan R. Kemp — *Abuse in the Family: An Introduction*. Pacific Grove, CA: Brooks/Cole, 1998.

Ethel Klein et al. — *Ending Domestic Violence: Changing Public Perceptions/Halting the Epidemic*. Thousand Oaks, CA: Sage Publications, 1997.

Renate C.A. Klein, ed. — *Multidisciplinary Perspectives on Family Violence*. New York: Routledge, 1998.

Kathryn Kuehnle — *Assessing Allegations of Child Sexual Abuse*. Sarasota, FL: Professional Resource Press, 1996.

Deborah Lockton and Richard Ward — *Domestic Violence*. London: Cavendish, 1997.

Amina Mama — *The Hidden Struggle: Statutory and Voluntary Sector Responses to Violence Against Black Women in the Home*. Concord, MA: Paul and Company Publishers Consortium, 1996.

James Ptacek — *Battered Women in the Courtroom: The Power of Judicial Responses*. Boston: Northeastern University Press, 1999.

Claire M. Renzetti and Charles H. Miley, eds. — *Violence in Gay and Lesbian Domestic Partnerships*. New York: Harrington Park, 1996.

Sherri L. Schornstein — *Domestic Violence and Health Care: What Every Professional Needs to Know*. Thousand Oaks, CA: Sage Publications, 1997.

Robert L. Snow — *Family Abuse: Tough Solutions to Stop the Violence*. New York: Plenum Press, 1997.

Ronald B. Taylor — *Preventing Violence Against Women and Children*. New York: Milbank Memorial Fund, 1997.

Harvey Wallace	*Family Violence: Legal, Medical, and Social Perspectives.* Boston: Allyn and Bacon, 1996.
K.J. Wilson	*When Violence Begins at Home: A Comprehensive Guide to Understanding and Ending Domestic Abuse.* Alameda, CA: Hunter House, 1997.
Cheryl Woodard	*Domestic Violence and Abuse: How to Stop It!* Occidental, CA: Nolo Press, 1996.

Periodicals

American Bar Association	"Lawyers Are Urged to Intervene to Help Victims of Domestic Abuse," *New York Times*, August 4, 1996.
American Medical Association	"AMA Guidelines for Doctors on Detecting Elder Abuse and Neglect," *Aging*, 1996 Special Edition.
Barbara Amiel	"The Real Problem in Handling Child Abuse," *Maclean's*, March 2, 1998.
Sandra R. Arbetter	"Family Violence," *Current Health*, November 1995.
Nina Bernstein	"Pattern Cited in Missed Signs of Child Abuse," *New York Times*, July 22, 1999.
Rosemary Black	"Domestic Violence: Why It's Every Woman's Issue . . . and What You Can Do," *American Health for Women*, March 1997.
Paul A. Blunt	"Financial Exploitation: The Best Kept Secret of Elder Abuse," *Aging*, 1996 Special Edition.
Rosemary Chalk and Patricia King	"Facing Up to Family Violence," *Issues in Science and Technology,* Winter 1998–1999.
Stephen Chapman	"Child Abuse: Politicians Shamelessly Exploit Children for Political Advantage," *The American Spectator*, June 1998.
Patricia Chisholm	"The Scourge of Wife Abuse," *Maclean's*, October 30, 1995.
Ellis Cose	"The Truth About Spouse Abuse," *Newsweek*, August 8, 1994.
James Cronin	"False Memory," *Z Magazine*, April 1994. Available from 116 S. Botolph St., Boston, MA 02115.
Susan Douglas	"Blame It on Battered Women," *Progressive*, August 1994.
Katherine Dunn	"Truth Abuse," *New Republic*, August 1, 1994.
Carey Goldberg	"Getting to the Truth in Child Abuse Cases: New Methods," *New York Times*, September 8, 1998.
Ted Guest with Betsy Streisand	"Still Failing Women?" *U.S. News & World Report*, June 19, 1995.
Philip J. Hilts	"Misdiagnoses Are Said to Mask Lethal Abuse," *New York Times*, September 11, 1997.
Marian M. Jones	"Battling Battering: Guidelines for Aiding Abused Female Co-workers," *Psychology Today*, November/December 1997.

Bibliography

John Leo — "Things That Go Bump in the Home: Women's Violence Against Men," *U.S. News & World Report*, May 13, 1996.

Hara E. Marano — "Why They Stay: A Saga of Spouse Abuse," *Psychology Today*, May/June 1996.

Alex Morales — "Seeking a Cure for Child Abuse," *USA Today*, September 1998.

Mary Ann Perga — "Marriage Is Not a Private Affair," *U.S. Catholic*, August 1996.

Martha R. Plotkin — "Improving the Police Response to Domestic Elder Abuse Victims," *Aging*, 1996 Special Edition.

Jennifer L. Rike — "Rage and Beyond," *Christian Century*, June 3, 1998.

Margaret Talbot — "Against Innocence: The Truth About Child Abuse and the Truth About Children," *The New Republic*, March 15, 1999.

Rosalie S. Wolf — "Understanding Elder Abuse and Neglect," *Aging*, 1996 Special Edition.

Cathy Young — "Abused Statistics," *National Review*, August 1, 1994.

Organizations to Contact

The editors have compiled the following list of organizations concerned with the issues debated in this book. The descriptions are derived from materials provided by the organizations. All have publications or information available for interested readers. The list was compiled on the date of publication of the present volume; names, addresses, and phone numbers may change. Be aware that many organizations take several weeks or longer to respond to inquiries, so allow as much time as possible.

Advocates for Abused and Battered Lesbians (AABL)
PO Box 85596, Seattle, WA 98105-9998
(206) 547-8191
e-mail: info@aabl.com • website: www.aabl.org

AABL provides services for lesbians and their children who are or have been victims of domestic violence. Through community education and outreach, its members encourage communities to recognize and eliminate lesbian battering, homophobia, and misogyny. AABL provides information on intimate abuse, and its website includes stories from survivors of domestic violence.

American Academy of Child and Adolescent Psychiatry (AACAP)
3615 Wisconsin Ave. NW, Washington, DC 20016-3007
(202) 966-7300 • fax: (202) 966-2891
website: www.aacap.org

AACAP is a nonprofit organization that supports and advances child and adolescent psychiatry through research and the distribution of information. The academy's goal is to provide information that will remove the stigma associated with mental illnesses and ensure proper treatment for children who suffer from mental or behavioral disorders due to child abuse, molestation, or other factors. AACAP publishes fact sheets on a variety of issues concerning disorders that may affect children and adolescents.

Center for the Prevention of Sexual and Domestic Violence (CPSDV)
936 N. 34th St., Suite 200, Seattle, WA 98013
(206) 634-1903 • fax: (206) 634-0115
e-mail: cpsdv@cpsdv.org • website: www.cpsdv.org

CPSDV is an educational resource center that works with both religious and secular communities throughout the United States and Canada to address issues of sexual abuse and domestic violence. The center offers workshops concerning clergy misconduct, spouse abuse, child sexual abuse, rape, and pornography. Materials available from CPSDV include training manuals, fact sheets, and the quarterly *Journal of Religion and Abuse*.

Childhelp USA
15757 N. 78th St., Scottsdale, AZ 85260
(480) 922-8212 • fax: (480) 922-7061
website: www.childhelpusa.org

Childhelp USA works toward the prevention and treatment of child abuse. The organization provides residential care and counseling services for abused and neglected children through its group and foster homes. It promotes public awareness of child abuse issues and offers a child abuse hotline that services North America. Its publications include the book *Child Abuse and You* and the periodic *Child Help Newsletter*.

False Memory Syndrome Foundation (FMSF)
3401 Market St., Suite 130, Philadelphia, PA 19104
(215) 387-1865 • fax: (215) 387-1917
e-mail: pjf@saul.cis.upenn.edu

FMSF believes that many "delayed memories" of sexual abuse are the result of false memory syndrome (FMS). In FMS, patients in therapy "recall" childhood abuse that never occurred. The foundation seeks to discover reasons for the spread of FMS, works for the prevention of new cases, and aids FMS victims, including those it believes have been falsely accused of abuse. FMSF publishes the *FMS Foundation Newsletter*, the booklet *The False Memory Syndrome Phenomenon*, and the books *Confabulations* and *True Stories of False Memories*.

Family Research Laboratory (FRL)
University of New Hampshire
126 Horton Social Science Center, Durham, NH 03824-3586
(603) 862-1888
website: www.unhinfo.unh.edu/frl

Since 1975, FRL has devoted itself primarily to understanding the causes and consequences of family violence and to working to dispel myths about family violence through public education. It publishes numerous books and articles on violence by men and women against their partners, the physical abuse of spouses or cohabitants, marital rape, and verbal aggression. Books available from FRL include *When Battered Women Kill* and *Physical Violence in American Families: Risk Factors and Adaptations to Violence in 8,145 Families*.

Family Violence Prevention Fund (FVPF)
383 Rhode Island St., Suite 304, San Francisco, CA 94103
(415) 252-8900 • fax: (415) 252-8991
website: www.fvpf.org

FVPF is a national nonprofit organization concerned with domestic violence education, prevention, and public policy reform. It works to improve health care for battered women and to strengthen the judicial system's capacity to respond appropriately to domestic violence cases. The fund publishes brochures, action kits, and general information packets on domestic violence as well as the books *Domestic Violence: The Law and Criminal Prosecution*, *Domestic Violence: The Crucial Role of the Judge in Criminal Court Cases*, and *Domestic Violence in Immigrant and Refugee Communities: Asserting the Rights of Battered Women*.

Feminist Majority Foundation
National Center for Women and Policing
8105 W. Third St., Los Angeles, CA 90048
(323) 651-2532 • fax: (323) 653-2689
e-mail: womencops@aol.com • website: www.feminist.org/police/ncwp.html

The center is a division of the Feminist Majority Foundation, an activist organization that works to eliminate sex discrimination and social and economic injustice. The center's members believe that female police officers respond more effectively to incidents of violence against women than do their male counterparts. It acts as a nationwide resource for law enforcement agencies and community leaders seeking to increase the number of female police officers in their communities and improve police response to family violence. The Feminist Majority Foundation publishes the quarterly *Feminist Majority Report*.

Focus on the Family
8605 Explorer Dr., Colorado Springs, CO 80995
(719) 531-3400

Focus on the Family believes that reestablishing the traditional two-parent family will end many social problems. The organization publishes the monthly magazine *Focus on the Family Citizen* and the resource list *Information on Abuse*, which lists books, audio tapes, and information sheets related to family violence.

Independent Women's Forum
PO Box 3058, Arlington, VA 22203-0058
(800) 224-6000 • (703) 558-4991 • fax: (703) 558-4994
e-mail: info@iwf.org • website: www.iwf.org

The forum is a conservative women's advocacy group that believes in individual freedom and personal responsibility and promotes common sense over feminist ideology. The forum believes that the incidence of domestic violence is exaggerated and that the Violence Against Women Act is ineffective and unjust. It publishes the journal *Women's Quarterly* and the *Ex Femina Newsletter*.

Metro Action Committee on Public Violence Against Women and Children (METRAC)
158 Spadina Rd., Toronto, ON M5R 2T8 CANADA
(416) 392-3135 • fax: (416) 392-3136
e-mail: metrac@interlog.com

METRAC works to prevent all forms of violence against women and children. It educates governments and the public about the harmful effects violence has on women, children, and the whole community. In addition, METRAC promotes research on violence, services for survivors, and legal system reform. Its publications include information packets and the books *Sexual Assault: A Guide to the Criminal System*, *Violence-Free Schools: Sexual Assault Prevention Manual*, and *Discussion Paper: Developing a Safe Urban Environment for Women*.

National Clearinghouse on Child Abuse and Neglect Information
330 C St. SW, Washington, DC 20447
(800) 394-3366 • (703) 385-7565 • fax: (703) 385-3206
website: www.calib.com/nccanch

This national clearinghouse collects, catalogs, and disseminates information on all aspects of child maltreatment, including identification, prevention, treatment, public awareness, training, and education. The clearinghouse offers various reports, fact sheets, and bulletins concerning child abuse and neglect.

National Coalition Against Domestic Violence (NCADV)
Child Advocacy Task Force
PO Box 18749, Denver, CO 80218-0749
(303) 839-1852 • fax: (303) 831-9251
website: www.ncadv.org

NCADV represents organizations and individuals that assist battered women and their children. The Child Advocacy Task Force deals with issues affecting children who witness violence at home or are themselves abused. It publishes various information pamphlets, community resource directories, and instruction manuals.

National Committee for the Prevention of Elder Abuse (NCPEA)
Institute on Aging
UMass Memorial Health Care
19 Belmont St., Worcester, MA 01605
(508) 793-6166 • fax: (508) 793-6906
e-mail: wolfr@memorialhc.org • website: www.mesacanada.com

The NCPEA seeks to increase public awareness of the problem of elder abuse and to foster the development of services to protect the elderly. Its programs include professional training, public advocacy, and academic research. The NCPEA publishes the quarterly *Journal of Elder Abuse and Neglect.*

National Resource Center on Child Sexual Abuse (NRCCSA)
107 Lincoln St., Huntsville, AL 35801
(800) 543-7006 • (205) 534-6868 • fax: (205) 534-6883

NRCCSA is funded by the National Center on Child Abuse and Neglect of the U.S. Department of Health and Human Services and is operated by the National Children's Advocacy Center. In addition to its toll-free information line, the center publishes a newsletter, information papers, monographs, and bibliographies on child abuse and neglect issues.

United Fathers of America (UFA)
6360 Van Nuys Blvd., Suite 8, Van Nuys, CA 91401
(818) 785-1440 • fax: (818) 995-0743
e-mail: info@unitedfathers.com • website: www.fathersunited.com
website: www.fathersforever.com (a branch of UFA)

UFA helps fathers fight for the right to remain actively involved in their children's upbringing after divorce or separation. UFA believes that children should not be subject to the emotional and psychological trauma caused when vindictive parents falsely charge ex-spouses with sexually abusing their children. Primarily a support group, UFA answers specific questions and suggests articles and studies that illustrate its position.

Women's Freedom Network (WFN)
4410 Massachusetts Ave. NW, Suite 179, Washington, DC 20016
(202) 885-6245
e-mail: rsimon@american.edu • website: www.womensfreedom.org

The network was founded in 1993 by a group of women who were seeking alternatives to both extremist ideological feminism and antifeminist traditionalism. It opposes gender bias in the sentencing of spouse abusers and believes acts of violence against women should be considered individually rather than stereotyped as gender-based hate crimes. WFN publishes a newsletter and the book *Neither Victim Nor Enemy: Women's Freedom Network Looks at Gender in America.*

Index

Index